About the Author

Frederick P. Hitz, author of *The Great Game: The Myths and Reality of Espionage* (2004) and *Unleashing the Rogue Elephant* (2002), was inspector general of the Central Intelligence Agency from 1990 to 1998. He teaches at the University of Virginia School of Law.

Why Spy?

Also by Frederick P. Hitz

The Great Game:
The Myths and Reality of Espionage

Unleashing the Rogue Elephant:
September 11 and Letting the CIA Be the CIA

Why Spy?

Espionage in an Age of Uncertainty

Frederick P. Hitz

THOMAS DUNNE BOOKS
St. Martin's Press
New York

All statements of fact, opinion, or analysis expressed are those of the author and do not reflect the official positions or views of the CIA or any other U.S. Government agency. Nothing in the contents should be construed as asserting or implying U.S. Government authentication of information or Agency endorsement of the author's views. This material has been reviewed by the CIA to prevent the disclosure of classified information.

THOMAS DUNNE BOOKS.
An imprint of St. Martin's Press.

WHY SPY? Copyright © 2008 by Frederick P. Hitz. All rights reserved. Printed in the United States of America. No part of this book may be used or reproduced in any manner whatsoever without written permission except in the case of brief quotations embodied in critical articles or reviews. For information, address St. Martin's Press, 175 Fifth Avenue, New York, N.Y. 10010.

www.thomasdunnebooks.com
www.stmartins.com

Book design by Kathryn Parise

LIBRARY OF CONGRESS CATALOGING-IN-PUBLICATION DATA

Hitz, Frederick Porter, 1939–
    Why spy? : espionage in an age of uncertainty / Frederick P. Hitz.–
1st ed.
        p.   cm.
    ISBN-13: 978-0-312-35604-0
    ISBN-10: 0-312-35604-8
    1. Intelligence service–United States.   2. Espionage, American.
3. United States. Central Intelligence Agency.   4. Espionage.   I. Title.
    JK468.I6H57 2008
    327.1273–dc22

                                                        2007039363

First Edition: April 2008

10   9   8   7   6   5   4   3   2   1

To the patriotic men and women of U.S. intelligence,
who work long and hard to protect this nation.
May they be given the leadership and support
that such a difficult task demands.

Contents

PART TWO
America's Spying Competence Today

PART THREE
Spying in the Twenty-first Century

PART FOUR
Why Spy? Should We Do It?

Acknowledgments

I want to acknowledge the invaluable assistance of my research assistant, Zack Hughes, Princeton '08, who helped me pull together a lot of the background information on the espionage cases cited in Part One, and checked facts in other parts of the manuscript. He was a volunteer for the enterprise and justified my confidence in his abilities. I hope to see him in public service one day.

I also acknowledge the helpful prodding and advice I received from Mark LaFlaur, senior editor at Thomas Dunne Books, who made numerous constructive suggestions on ways to reorder, amplify points, and otherwise tighten up the manuscript during its preparation. Both he and Tom Dunne have made it a better book.

Introduction

Everyone knows that generals and admirals prepare to fight the next war based on the doctrine, practices, and lessons learned from the last one. This is human nature. We all tend to rely on what we know best and what has worked in the past.

Can this be true in espionage as well? Do the experience gained and the lessons learned in cold war spying carry over to a time of holy terror, when the gatherers of intelligence are targeting suicide bombers and an unstructured alliance, Al Qaeda (Arabic for "the base") dedicated to driving Western powers out of the Middle East? That is the question posed in this work, because the president and Congress have made a big bet in passing the Intelligence Reform and Terrorism Prevention Act of 2004 that a revitalization of human source intelligence, i.e., traditional spying, is critical to the prevention of future 9/11s.

Both the 9/11 Commission and the Silberman-Robb Commission on the Intelligence Capabilities of the United States Regarding Weapons of Mass Destruction studying the Iraqi weapons of mass destruction (WMD) intelligence failures have concluded that an absence of well-placed human sources on the ground was directly responsible in a major way for these disasters. The president and Congress concurred in these judgments, and are determined to reconstruct and revitalize U.S. spying capabilities against terrorist targets. Iran, North Korea, China, and perhaps India are also prominent intelligence targets in the new millennium. There is thus little discernible dissent from the conclusion that U.S. spying must improve.

The real question is, of course, how to do it.

Will the old-time religion of spotting, assessing, developing, and recruiting agents by spy handlers operating from positions in official installations abroad be successful against Islamist fundamentalists and others, as it was against the Soviets during the cold war, or are there new lessons to be learned in operating against the new national targets and a formless, nonstate band of fanatics promoting an "ism"? Surely our experience thus far in operating against Osama bin Laden, the insurrectionists in Iraq, and North Korea suggests the latter. I will explore how.

At present, the administration and Congress appear to have concluded that more money and spy runners are the answer.[1] The president has charged the director of the Central Intelligence Agency with increasing the cadre of U.S. case officers by 50 percent. This is based on an assumption that *humint* (as human source intelligence is called in the federal bureaucracy) was permitted to atrophy in the years following the end of the cold war in 1991, and needs a special infusion of support to get back on track. The further assumption made by the president and Congress is that if a new investment in additional human resources is made, coupled with a reinforced emphasis on speaking the difficult languages of the Middle East and East Asia (which is also to be bumped up to produce 50 percent more difficult-language speakers), we will soon be in a position to steal the information needed to avoid future 9/11s and Iraqi WMD intelligence fiascoes.

This book will question whether that optimism is well-founded or merely represents the latest instance in which Washington, D.C., seeks to solve a problem by throwing money at it. Can the lessons learned about spying in the cold war be reworked to lead to success in a time of jihadism, antiglobalization, and increasing anti-Americanism? Do the motivations to spy for the West remain relevant—the desire to grasp freedom and spread prosperity—or are they effectively blocked by concerns about a new crusade and foreign exploitation of oil wealth? Are they confused by our understandings of freedom and democracy that do not comport with those of Islam or the cultures of East Asia?

There are seven classic motivations to commit espionage—ideology, money, revenge, blackmail, friendship, ethnic or religious solidarity, and love of espionage for its own sake. Exploring how these reasons for spying hold up under today's conditions, we shall also examine whether the U.S. spying apparatus is configured optimally to perform the espionage mission today and whether we are attracting and retaining the best people to perform this mission. Finally, I will address the question of whether human source intelli gence gathering—humint—is destined to play much of a role in countering international threats to the United States in the twenty-first century. Can we get most of what we need to know to support the president's national security policy tech nologically or through the open literature? Do we really *need* spies anymore?

It may be useful at the outset to describe how the United States goes about its espionage mission. If we had chosen to design a perfect system of intelligence gathering, analysis, and dissemination in 1947, when the CIA was created after World War II, it would hardly resemble the hodgepodge of disparate functions and agencies that have today grown to sixteen: the self-described intelligence community (IC). A more oxy moronic label than "community" is not to be found in Wash ington. According to recent newspaper reports, the IC numbers approximately 100,000 employees and ostensibly re ports to a director of National Intelligence (DNI) created by the Intelligence Reform and Terrorism Prevention Act of 2004. It encompasses the Central Intelligence Agency (CIA), the Federal Bureau of Investigation (FBI), and the Defense In telligence Agency (DIA) that are the principal spy agencies of the U.S. government that engage in human source intelligence collection, i.e., classic espionage, about which this work will be largely concerned. The other principal IC members are the National Security Agency (NSA), the National Reconnais sance Office (NRO), the National Geospatial Intelligence

Agency (NGIA), the Department of Homeland Security (DHS), the Drug Enforcement Administration (DEA), the Department of State's Bureau of Intelligence and Research (INR), and the intelligence offices of the military departments— Army, Navy, Air Force, and Marines. These organizations all perform specialized technological intelligence functions— signals and electronic intelligence by NSA; satellite reconnaissance by the NRO; image and photo interpretation by the NGIA—or perform departmental intelligence functions for discrete constituencies. That is true of the intelligence offices of the Treasury and Energy departments that provide specialized expertise, and the Justice Department that makes sure it is all legal. Finally, the office of the DNI itself makes sixteen. This is far too broad and diverse an assemblage over which to expect one official to exercise operational or budgetary control, but we shall get to that question later.

Part One

The Seven Motivations for Espionage

Chapter One

Espionage versus Intelligence:
How the United States Goes About Spying

Before discussing in detail why spies choose to spy, we ought to figure out what espionage is and how the United States goes about it. Spying has a long history, stretching back to biblical times. Tribes, ethnicities, and other authorities have always wanted to know what their enemies or rivals were planning to do to them or how they might act to protect a perceived vital interest. If the rival power refused to share the information, it had to be stolen or suborned. The High Priest's minions sought to bribe Judas Iscariot, one of Jesus' followers, into revealing the prophet's whereabouts so they could eliminate him before Rome interfered to bring Jerusalem to heel.

In medieval and renaissance times, spies infiltrated the courts of rival kingdoms and principalities to acquire the secrets that might undermine them or keep them at a safe distance—and they were called ambassadors.

George Washington believed strongly in the value of intelligence. He arrived at an understanding with the Continental Congress in 1775 that it would create a separate secret committee, the Committee of Secret Correspondence, whose mission it would be to furnish General Washington with unvouchered, unaccountable funds that he could spend to hire spies to protect the Continental Army. One of those spies, an untutored but enthusiastic young schoolmaster, Nathan Hale, volunteered to go behind the British lines on Long Island in 1776 to spy, but he was so green that he was immediately captured and hanged. Although he was clearly temperamentally unsuited for espionage, Hale had been willing to try it because his country and fellow soldiers so desperately needed intelligence about the British Army's plans and whereabouts in New York.

I once heard Reagan administration director of Central Intelligence William J. Casey remark, as he walked past the statue of Nathan Hale implanted beside the main entrance to the original CIA headquarters building in Langley, Virginia, that he'd like to replace Hale with a statue of Hercules Mulligan. Unlike Hale, Casey noted, Mulligan was a successful spy throughout the American Revolution. Like Hale, a Yale graduate, Mulligan was a member of Washington's Committee of Secret Correspondence from 1775 until the end of the Revolutionary War. He successfully spied for Washington in New York City, once crossing through enemy lines carrying a letter from Alexander

Hamilton outlining the best way to evacuate outgunned American troops from Long Island. Mulligan's clothing business and his brother's export-import firm permitted close contact with senior officers in the British Army occupying New York, and Mulligan took full advantage of these relationships to gather tidbits concerning British troop movements and plans. He successfully warned of a British plan to capture General Washington in 1779, and a later plan to interdict his passage to New England in 1781. Mulligan lived until 1825, having known many of the principal figures from New York on the American side during the revolution. He was a champion of the cause of American freedom spurred by a principled distaste for British rule, owing in no small part to his Irish heritage. That is doubtless what appealed to Director Casey.

More recently, in the late nineteenth and early twentieth centuries, Britain and other colonial powers used espionage to defend empire. "The Great Game," as Kipling called it, was employed to prevent the czarist Russians and their French allies from interfering with Britain's economic and political domination of the Indian subcontinent. Britain sought to train natives, or white sahibs who could pass for natives, to hang out in the bazaars or go on surveying missions in the outback to keep track of hostile efforts to undermine its influence.

In World War I, Britain used its skill in breaking foreign diplomatic codes to intercept German radio messages threatening interference with neutral shipping in the North Atlantic, or planning an alliance with Mexico to return territory "stolen" from it by the United States during the Mexican-American War. These messages, including the famous Zimmermann

Telegram, were secretly shared with President Wilson to lay the groundwork for his decision to enter the war on the allied side in 1917. Here was modern technology employed to enhance the espionage effort against hostile communications of enemy states that the collector then used very effectively to get help for its cause.

The period between the wars saw a lot of espionage for hire, as varied newly enfranchised states in central Europe and the Middle East sought to establish themselves and protect their independence but did not have the experience or money to pay for an intelligence service of their own. The rise of fascism led to efforts by the Axis powers to infiltrate the West, including the United States, where J. Edgar Hoover was finally instructed by President Roosevelt in 1940 to go after Nazi plans to sabotage U.S. cargo bound for European ports. This was the first recognition that the United States was disadvantaged by not having a peacetime civilian intelligence service, and led to the chartering of the Office of Strategic Services (OSS) under General William "Wild Bill" Donovan during World War II, and the Central Intelligence Agency (CIA) in 1947. In between, of course, the United States had suffered the shocking disaster of the Pearl Harbor attack in December 1941, about which we had had no intelligence warning. In the postwar postmortems about the event it was hotly debated as to whether this was a failure of collection or analysis, but in the end, an otherwise skeptical President Truman was convinced that the United States needed a civilian spy service, and the CIA was created.

This brings us to the era of modern espionage. The charter of the fledgling CIA in 1947 was to become the action element in the U.S. government to respond to George Kennan's clarion call to oppose the westward drive of the postwar Soviet empire, the policy of containment. The CIA was empowered to do this by spying and by covert political operations ("covert action"), which ran the gamut from black propaganda (where the source of the propaganda is hidden) to funding democratic political parties in Italy and elsewhere; to sending in sabotage teams behind the Iron Curtain to roll back communism. It was a mammoth assignment and a gigantic project, which neither the State nor Defense departments wanted to take on, so it fell to the new kid on the block. After a very slow start in the late forties it began to succeed, turning into a meaningful effort to penetrate and infiltrate Soviet agent networks in the West, in the mid-sixties. The Soviets, of course, had been quite successful in launching espionage operations against its future allies in the West beginning in the mid-1930s, before the war, and continuing with the successful effort to steal U.S. atomic secrets, which led to the testing of a Soviet nuclear bomb in 1948, five years in advance of most intelligence predictions.

We shall concentrate on the legacy of espionage operations mounted by Western intelligence agencies against the Soviet Union during the cold war period that ran from 1946 to 1991, to establish the baseline of knowledge about espionage for comparison with the current challenges posed by Islamist terrorism. The reason for this is clear. For forty-five years, this was the principal mission of U.S. intelligence agencies. This is what we had to learn to do after the CIA was chartered in 1947 at the outset of the cold war, and how we learned it.

Covert action (political operations where the hand of the United States is intended not to show) will also be considered, because this was also a critical part of the CIA's mission. Yet it is my view, after observing the extent to which it has become impossible under current circumstances of around-the-clock worldwide media coverage, the Internet, and expanded congressional oversight to mount these operations in secrecy, that they are likely to play but a small part in the intelligence war on terrorism. In sum, we shall be looking principally at what the United States knows about human spy operations.

Nonetheless, we shall not restrict our inquiry to cloak-and-dagger operations, dead drops, and microdots alone. America has made many contributions to universal spycraft,[1] but its greatest over the years are perhaps in the realm of sophisticated communications technology, i.e., satellite reconnaissance and eavesdropping, and electronic surveillance. We shall want to see how these technical aids will help the West follow international money transfers and Internet communications among terrorist cells. We shall need to understand better the possibilities of using modern computers to capture and analyze reams of data, i.e., data mining.

Nonetheless, the principal focus of our inquiry is a question of human behavior and motivation. Why do spies spy?

To begin, we have to define what spies do. I have borrowed in the past from Kim Philby's definition of espionage as the collection of "secret information from foreign countries by illegal means."[2] I am no longer sure that this epigrammatic formulation gets it all. For example, calling information "secret" suggests that there is a requirement that it be formally adjudged to be so, and be so stamped. In reality, we don't care about definitions. We are concerned with information that the spy wants to obtain and that the owner of it wants to protect, regardless of its intrinsic sensitivity.

Second, the spy universe is no longer adequately defined by "foreign *countries*." It includes Al Qaeda or the Taliban or the Iraqi insurgents or the Kosovar Serbs or the rebels of Darfur—whatever transnational group is engaged in hostile action against Western interests.

Finally, "illegal means" is too polite, too marquis of Queensbury. We are talking about stealing secrets. This is no parlor game but a down and dirty effort, electronic or human, to get at the intentions of the enemy, to strip his cupboard bare.

That is what makes the core question of why spies spy so compelling. However the spy may dress it up or the good spy runner may sugarcoat it, a spy is betraying a trust. He or she is revealing to a third party information that he or she, his friends, family, and professional associates are prohibited from sharing. It is an act that has consequences, as we shall note. And herein lies the essential conundrum of the present time. If spying is an enterprise so fraught with fundamental risk, can we be confident that simply hiring more case officers and teaching them hard languages will accomplish the task? Aren't there additional parts to the equation? If so, what might they be? What are the motivations for espionage that can be learned and that might be exploited to give some hope of success against the practitioners of martyrdom operations?

Espionage is distinguished from other forms of intelligence gathering by its clandestinity and its "illegal means" of acquisition. Spies are traitors who can be shot for their transgressions, as can the case officers who run them if they are not diplomats. Not all intelligence reports provided daily to the president are derived from stolen secret information provided by spies. Much of it is open source information acquired by experts in the course of perusing Web sites, media outlets, academic monographs, and conversations with other experts who know the region or subject being explicated. It is derived from ambassadorial and foreign service officer reports from American embassies abroad and military attachés serving in them. In fact, about 95 percent of most intelligence reports that reach the president's desk are largely derived from sources that, if you knew what you were looking for, would be openly available. It becomes intelligence by virtue of the expertise of the analyst who pulls all source information together in a way that explains the meaning and implications of an event to the president and his top policy makers. No espionage may be involved.

During World War II, the CIA's predecessor, the Office of Strategic Services (OSS), was given credit for having invented something called "all-source intelligence analysis" that combined fragments of information from newspapers, academic journals, legal travelers, and spies to present to the nation's top decision makers as complete a picture of ball-bearing production in Nazi Germany, let's say, as was available anywhere.

Note that even at that time, these analysts did not have access to intercepted wire or radio communications, more commonly known in the trade as *sigint*. That was reserved for military intelligence agencies. The OSS analysts were often postdoctorates or young faculty from distinguished universities, and they were putting in their daily dozen or fourteen hours a day to track the efforts of the Axis powers to feed their war machine. Even from these hoary beginnings the lion's share of basic intelligence collection and analysis was derived from ingenious, dogged research in open source materials enriched by the occasional clandestine report that clarified some aspect of what the analyst was looking for or at.

To be sure, the clandestinely acquired 5 percent of intelligence information is often the nugget or key fact that gives the report salience or authenticity. But it does not necessarily dominate the interpretation, meaning, or significance of the piece.

The second aspect of the secret 5 percent is that it might not be (and usually isn't) derived from humint—human spies. It can be sigint or overhead satellite photography. It could also be the report of a cooperating foreign intelligence liaison service.

Therefore, human spying and intelligence gathering and analysis are not synonymous. Most good intelligence is a pastiche of various bits of information put together authoritatively by analysts with deep knowledge of the subject area where the clandestinely acquired pieces are but a part, perhaps the most important part, but only a part of the whole. Humint is unlikely to be a high volume or comfortably predictable part of the entire intelligence collection enterprise. In the past I have called espionage "pick and shovel" work: tedious, slow, unpredictable, but vitally important, because it can often lead the analyst to information he may not be able to acquire elsewhere, information about a subject's *intentions*.[3]

Next we need to know who in the U.S. government does the spying. Of the sixteen separate intelligence agencies that make up the U.S. intelligence community noted earlier, only two are supposed to have spy runners on the ground collecting human source intelligence overseas.[4] They are the CIA and the Defense Humint Service. CIA's directorate of operations (DO) has been in charge of spying since the agency was created in 1947, and before that as OSS during World War II. Its targets have traditionally been political and economic intelligence of national interest to the president and his chief policy makers. The DO is also responsible for covert action (CA) as directed by the president and the National Security Council.

The Defense Humint Service is a relatively new entrant in the field of foreign espionage, having been created in 1993 after the 1991 Gulf War to organize the military's effort to gather tactical intelligence around the battlefield for purposes of aiding and protecting U.S. forces fighting abroad. It replaced the individual efforts of the military services and the defense attaché's offices. The CIA remains the manager of national humint collection, meaning Defense Humint Service officers are supposed to coordinate their collection efforts with the senior CIA representative in the field. With the proliferation of antiterrorist intelligence collection efforts abroad, however, this coordination has been harder to come by.

A word must be said about the FBI in this connection. Except for a short period during World War II, the FBI has largely confined its spying efforts to the domestic scene. With the growing importance of antiterrorist activity, and the disappearance of a distinction between foreign and domestic terrorist planning and operations, the FBI has built up its presence in legal attaché offices in U.S. embassies abroad from which it is not supposed to run espionage operations; but FBI agents do involve themselves with friendly foreign intelligence liaison services in antiterrorist issues of common concern.

Finally, why do we need to do this at all? How much information essential to the protection of the West from future suicide bombings is actually secret and cannot be acquired by studious data mining of the Internet or good investigative police work? This has traditionally been a tough question to answer, but may be less so given the offensive posture most Western leaders want their intelligence and domestic security agencies to assume. The goal now is to prevent another 9/11, Madrid train bombing, or 7/7 London Underground attack from occurring, not just finding out who did it after the fact. If intelligence and domestic security are in a preemptive and preventive mode, they will need accurate and timely intelligence about future attacks before they occur, which means penetrating the terrorist cells while they are still planning the attacks.

Obviously, today's is a new world for espionage, but cold

war successes include several instances where timely intelligence about a then current state of mind helped Western leaders avoid a disaster. A clear example is the intelligence information provided to President John F. Kennedy in October 1962 by U.S./U.K. spy Colonel Oleg Penkovsky during the Cuban missile crisis. Penkovsky reported that Soviet general secretary Nikita Khrushchev had not been fully supported in the Politburo and the General Staff in his decision to introduce intermediate-range ballistic missiles (IRBMs) into Cuba. That nugget, confirmed by former U.S. ambassador to the Soviet Union Llewelyn Thompson, sitting at Kennedy's side, gave the president the room he needed to attempt a different strategy from that being urged on him by the U.S. military. Instead of bombing Cuba into the stone age to take advantage of the fact that our U-2 spy planes had provided us with clear evidence of Soviet missile installations on the island, and that the Soviets did not yet know that we knew, President Kennedy decided to give Khrushchev an opportunity to step back from a confrontation that might have led to the beginning of World War III. He gave away the advantage of a surprise bombing in favor of a strategy of "quarantine," or embargo, to give Khrushchev an opportunity to reverse an impulsive decision not supported by his own military and political leaders.

The successful resolution of the Cuban missile crisis is an example of timely intelligence information permitting a Western political leader to act carefully before he might have been forced to embark upon a radical course of action that might lead to war, or accept a fait accompli. This is what the political leaders of Western democracies expect their intelligence and domestic security services to provide every day against potential terrorist attack. As former director of central intelligence George Tenet observed after September 11, in the intelligence business, a .350 batting average won't do; you've got to bat 1.000. Unfortunately, this rate of success is infrequent, if not impossible.

Furthermore, access to this kind of intelligence will be far more difficult in an era of Islamist terrorism. The groups that have formed to mount suicide attacks against the West are not nation-states yet. They are not subject to pressure from their peers if they go over the line. Their actions cannot be condemned before the community of nations in the UN as Ambassador Stevenson did with the Soviets in 1962, showing the world the U-2 photographic evidence of the Soviet IRBM installations on Cuba. Instead, Al Qaeda looks to many observers like a terrorist franchising operation, providing money and know-how to local bands who plan to attack local targets. Its ranks appear to be continually replenished by like-minded radical Islamists throughout the Muslim world. In this way, the terrorists are operating worldwide more like individual cells, taking advantage of targets of opportunity, and susceptible perhaps to penetration by local law enforcement more than by national intelligence entities.

In any event, if the West is to be successful against this new wave of holy terror, it will have to penetrate the terrorists' inner sanctum and steal their plans, and it will have to make use of every sophisticated surveillance capability in its arsenal to detect the perpetrators.

This will, of course, bring other ramifications. Civil libertarians may be shocked at the changes called for to gather preemptive intelligence against terrorists: longer periods of administrative detention for terrorist suspects; more intrusive surveillance techniques used against suspects; and elimination of privacy protections. This has certainly been the reaction in some quarters of the U.S. to passage of the USA Patriot Act, particularly in light of the fact that we have had the good fortune to escape further large-scale attacks since September 11, 2001.

That, however, is not the subject of this work. Recognizing the enormity of today's challenge, what we want to know is how well our past experience during the cold war has prepared us to penetrate the inner councils of the jihadists. Which of the vulnerabilities described as the seven motivations for espionage in the following pages can be exploited to gain the intelligence information we need to protect us against a suicide bomber? Why have spies worked for us in the past, and why might they spy for us now? And what might be our chances of success in an era of Islamist terror?

Chapter Two

Ideological Commitment

C ase officers sent abroad to gather intelligence information for the United States are for the most part not themselves spies. They are not the stuff of John Buchan, Ian Fleming, or Tom Clancy novels, where the protagonist and hero is the spy himself. They might be in time of war and in other special circumstances, but primarily, real case officers are empowered to *recruit* and *run* spies, hence my preference for the terms "spy runner" or "spy handler."

The reasons for this are quite logical. Most Americans have no possibility of infiltrating a terrorist cell or Wahhabite madrassa. They don't look like Iraqis, Afghanis, or Pakistanis, and sadly, they don't begin to speak the local languages well enough. Their assignment is to pick out and make the acquaintance of individuals who *do* have the entrée to these restricted target circles. Or find local collaborators in the host intelligence service who will help them do so. It is an extremely difficult assignment, especially when one considers the low state of opinion toward the West held by many Middle Easterners today. Yet I believe it can be done if we adapt and modify the techniques we used to recruit spies against the Soviet Union during the cold war. At least we will not be spending inordinate amounts of time just getting physically close to our target subjects. The USSR was a closed society for the greater part of the twentieth century, so meeting and assessing potential Soviet friends was a highly complicated, time-consuming task.

The first point of approach to a potential spy might be ideological. What philosophical and political interests does a targeted individual possess that are compatible to the recruiter's interests or can be made to appear so?

This was the genius of Soviet recruiters in the 1930s, approaching the intelligentsia of Britain and the United States in the midst of the Great Depression. They could point to a massive failure of the U.S./European capitalist model, with all the innocent people thrown out of work because of the alleged greed of Wall Street speculators. They could cite the remarkable strides being made in socialist Russia, building a worker-peasant partnership that was lifting the Soviet Union out of the feudalism of the czars to become a modern industrial state in two generations. Men like the infamous Cambridge Five at Trinity College, Cambridge, in the mid-1930s observed waiters at the dinner table stuffing their pockets with crusts of bread while the toffs discussed Keynes's latest economic theory to get the country back on its feet, and were disgusted. American sympathizers like Michael Straight were appalled by the unemployed Welsh coal miners who knocked at the rooms of Trinity in the evening, begging for a quid or two to send home to desperate families in Cardiff.

Similar kinds of contacts were being made in New Deal Washington. Alger Hiss at State, Harry Dexter White at Treasury, and Laughlin Currie in the White House were Soviet sympathizers, later spies, who were initially drawn to Soviet communism by the contrast between the depredations of Western capitalism in the 1930s and the promise of the USSR.

Some on both sides of the Atlantic woke up when word arrived of Stalin's systematic purges of his Bolshevik allies, beginning with his political rivals in 1936 and continuing through the Red Army, the diplomatic corps, and the predecessor of the KGB during the early years of World War II. These purges claimed the lives of an estimated thirteen million Russians. If this did not open some eyes, then the Molotov–von Ribbentrop Pact of 1939, allying the USSR with Nazi Germany in the dismemberment of the Baltics and parts of Eastern Europe, certainly did, for those whose commitment to Soviet communism was blindly idealistic.

Despite the argument of a recent biography of Michael Straight, for example, I believe these latter events terminated any lingering chance that Mr Straight would in the end become an espionage agent of the USSR in the Roosevelt administration.[1] For this is the coda in the recruitment of spies based on ideology. If, upon examination, the ideology itself cannot bear the burden of its adherents' beliefs, the recruitments will sour and come to naught. Consider the turning of two important low-level American communists, Soviet agents Whittaker Chambers and Elizabeth Bentley. At the onset of World War II, when they became convinced that the Stalinist purges might entrap them, they both decided to approach the FBI with full confessions of their spy activities rather than wait for the hammer to fall. Or there was the decision of Jay Lovestone to spend the rest of his life fighting Soviet communism after Stalin blocked his ascension to the head of the American Communist Party in 1929.

There is a considerable gap between commitment to an ideology, even one that espouses the violent overthrow of a government to which one owes allegiance, and the commitment actually to spy under the direction and control of a foreign power. Lines are crossed there with which the idealist will have difficulty. My belief is that Michael Straight may have been a communist in his sympathies while at Dartington Hall, the London School of Economics, and at Cambridge, where he took a double first in economics under John Maynard Keynes. However, when at Anthony Blunt's suggestion, the Soviets tried to pull the string on him when he returned to the United States to work at the State Department, he produced several classified memos but did not agree to a long-term agent relationship. Naïve and opposed to confrontation as he may have been, Straight's political sympathies did not extend so far as to permit him to become the servant of Stalin's imperialism.

Ryszard Kuklinski volunteered his services to the U.S. government in 1972 from a position high in the Polish Defense Ministry.[2] From this position, for nine years he supplied top Warsaw Pact plans for the movement of troops west in the event of an outbreak of war. Kuklinski was a highly regarded Polish Army staff officer who had a bright future in his own service. So what caused him to volunteer to spy for the Americans at enormous risk to himself and his beloved family?

Quite simply, he convinced himself that his cooperation with the CIA was the only way he could counter Soviet domination of Poland, its army, and the Solidarity movement. He saw himself as a Polish nationalist who took the only road open to him to save his country. Only by entrusting his country's defense and its defense secrets to the Americans could he prevent Poland from becoming the doormat over which the first Soviet military steps would be taken in the event of an outbreak of war. Enduring the danger and inconvenience of loading and unloading dead drops to pass and receive information in the cold and snow of a Warsaw winter, his motivation to take such risks had to have been forged of a strong belief in the rightness of his course. Likewise, he engaged in brush passes by automobile, exchanging intelligence with CIA officials which if spotted by Polish intelligence would have ended his career forthwith. It was a clandestine relationship that could only have been sustained by Kuklinski if he had a firm conviction that he was doing the right thing. Was there an easier or more effective way? Did Kuklinski have to violate his oath as an officer in the Polish Army and betray his fellow officers?

As Kuklinski soon discovered after the Americans could no longer protect him and exfiltrated him and his family to the United States in 1982, the Polish government and his fellow officers did not consider him a patriot. They believed he took the easy way out, escaping to the United States as Poland submitted to occupation and the imposition of martial law by the Soviets. After the collapse of communism in 1991, it took the intervention of President Jimmy Carter's national security advisor Zbigniew Brzezinski, among others, to get Kuklinski officially rehabilitated in noncommunist Poland. In the meantime, although Kuklinski and his wife and two sons were well provided for by the CIA in the United States, their lives were not without sorrow. For example, although they were both mature adults, both sons found difficulties in rerooting themselves in American soil, perishing in separate accidents relatively soon after their arrival in the United States. The point is that although the CIA considered Kuklinski to be a heroic spy because of the enormity and steadfastness of his contributions to American national security, such heroism is clearly in the eye of the beholder. Many of his former colleagues in Poland did not feel the same way. If it had not been for his longtime CIA friend and case officer, David Forden, there is no way this operation would have survived the grinding effects of the tension and risk under which Kuklinski operated for as long as he did. Forden communicated with him regularly even when Forden was on assignment in other countries—maintaining his interest as a friend and appreciative collaborator in Kuklinski's mission to save Poland from the Russian bear. This continual infusion of unconditional support and understanding made it so that in his own eyes Kuklinski could justify the unusual course he had chosen. This, despite the certain recriminations of his unwitting colleagues, who would consider him a traitor even though they might also detest the Soviets. In the circumstances of espionage and betrayal, one country's heroic spy is another's traitor.

A similar analysis can be made of Adolf Tolkachev, a Soviet official in military research and development of sophisticated weaponry.[3] He volunteered to spy for the United States by placing esoteric messages in U.S. diplomatic-plated automobiles near the U.S. Embassy in Moscow in the 1980s. At great personal risk, he brought out of his office reams of classified documents about Soviet air defense systems and antimissile defenses. In so doing, he saved the American taxpayer untold millions in unnecessary defense expenditures, because with Tolkachev's stolen intelligence, the United States was able to avoid certain blind-alley offensive measures it had been prepared to invest in if it believed the USSR was headed that way. To the United States, Tolkachev is another heroic spy who deplored the excessive war-making preparations of his nation while neglecting critical domestic needs. More important for the United States, he was willing to do something to prevent the USSR from gaining a military advantage over the West.

At the same time, in a seeming contradiction for an ideological spy, Tolkachev was a very proud individual who asked the United States to set aside money to pay him for his espionage, as if he were a high-priced defense consultant in Washington, D.C. It wasn't that he was greedy, or that he could envision any opportunity to spend the money. Tolkachev merely wanted some concrete measure of the value of his information to U.S. intelligence. I believe it is also a sign that despite all of the steps taken by the CIA to assure Tolkachev of the value of his contribution to the West, and the high regard in which he was held, he knew he was a spy and a traitor, and that he was entitled to some compensation for the risks he was taking and the value of the information he was providing, especially after his access dried up and he was of no further use to us. In any event, Tolkachev was probably betrayed by both Edward Lee Howard and Aldrich Ames, and was one of the ten Soviets spying for the United States caught by the KGB and summarily executed based on Ames's information.

Not everyone involved in the spy game in a significant position believes that the "heroic spy" who betrays his country for "pure" ideological motives is the genuine article. Russia's great spy master Viktor Cherkashin, who handled both CIA spy Aldrich Ames and FBI spy Robert Hanssen, has written recently that in his experience, no spy ever betrayed his country and friends for purely ideological reasons.[4] Cherkashin maintains that there is always something more involved.

Where does ideology take you in a time of jihadist terror? Are there spies like Kuklinski and Tolkachev lurking among the Islamist fundamentalists, willing to betray their cells and coreligionists to prevent the imposition of a fourteenth-century caliphate? Will they believe as Kuklinski and Tolkachev evidently did about their Soviet leaders, that Osama and his top lieutenants are offering a poisoned cup that will prevent the Arab world from realizing its modern potential? How do we identify such individuals? Will they be courageous enough to drop a note in a U.S. diplomat's car as Tolkachev did? All current indications are that it will be a tremendous feat just to lay the groundwork for such a possibility. There are few face-to-face opportunities for Islamist radicals to converse with Westerners under circumstances where there is not a shooting war taking place or a struggle over alleged Western incursion in the Middle East. The ideal contact, of course, would be with a leader who shares Islamist goals for a rebirth of the power and prestige of Muslim identity and culture in the Middle East but believes that the imposition of sharia law and the continued opposition to empowerment of women are the wrong paths to follow. The biggest knot to undo might well be the corruption of the Koranic ideal of *jihad* as encouraging martyrdom by suicide bombing. At present, there is no sign that Muslim clerics who dispute the terrorists' interpretation of *jihad* and martyrdom are willing to stand up in any numbers and call for a different interpretation. Quite the opposite. The evidence suggests that those imams willing to oppose jihad and martyrdom operations against the West are subject to *takfir,* denunciation as apostates by the jihadist militants.

Soviet Communism also enjoyed a brief vogue in the 1930s of appearing to be the antidote for unbridled and exploitative capitalism.

Time revealed its true face. The same thing may happen to Islamist fundamentalism, as increasing numbers of inhabitants of the Middle East come to recognize that a holy war based on terroristic attack on innocent civilians is not a formula for progress in attracting investment and meeting economic and population demands in the region. It is only negative. Western intelligence may be successful in recruiting some of the dissidents who oppose Wahhabism and Salafism, but it will require far more contact with the movers and shakers in this arena than we currently enjoy.

Furthermore, this struggle is more likely to be joined, at least at the outset, in the public domain than in the secret world of classic espionage operations. To be sure, Western nations and their allies in the Middle East are vigorously seeking intelligence information to disrupt and preempt future terrorist attacks; but it is more likely to be developed as a consequence of greater physical and electronic surveillance at international borders, in subways, and in radical mosques than it is from human penetration of small radical cells. In that sense, we shall see an increasing interdependence between foreign intelligence services like the CIA and Britain's MI-6, with their domestic security partners, the FBI, MI-5, and local police forces. Such successes as we may enjoy in this new enterprise will likely come as a consequence of timely and accurate forensics and excellent police work, rather than cloak-and-dagger operations. Furthermore, as we have seen in the criticisms mounted by the 9/11 Commission, this intelligence information will have to be instantly and widely shared, so immigration officials and first responders will be in a position to act. This will, of course, necessitate for the CIA and FBI and their foreign counterparts the alteration of a lifetime of professional habits. Compartmentation and grand jury secrecy and "need to know" may be preserved in certain instances to protect the name of a critical source, but they must be cast aside when it is a question of preventing a suicide bombing attack. On this issue of creating an information sharing environment, there is still a long road to travel, despite the efforts set forth in statute in the U.S. Intelligence Reform and Terrorism Prevention Act of 2004 to mandate it.

I can think of one outstanding recent success in applying this new imperative of information sharing, and it was in a case of domestic terrorism in the United States. It was also initially unintended. During the autumn of 2002, two snipers went on a rampage, killing innocent shoppers and passersby in a series of randomly targeted shootings. (Ten were killed and three injured in the Maryland and Virginia suburbs of Washington, D.C. Six others were killed across the nation.) Eventually, the local police got a firm fix on the make, model, and color of the sniper vehicle from witnesses to the early killings. There was extended debate in the police command center in Montgomery County, Maryland, as to the wisdom of releasing this information to the public, because it was feared the snipers might hear it and change vehicles. In the end, whether by intention or because of a mistake, the Maryland State Police broadcast the snipers' car description over the police radio band, and an alert interstate truck driver took the info over his CB just as he passed a Maryland public rest area on a major highway. He spotted the car parked. He stopped, blocked the ingress and egress to the rest area, called the state police, and the snipers were apprehended asleep in the vehicle. This strikes me as a perfect example of a coming truism in a time of international jihadist terror. Intelligence agencies and police will have to trust other government agencies and the public to handle time-sensitive terrorist prevention information sensibly if we are to successfully cope with the terrorists' reliance on surprise and randomness.

Chapter Three

Money and Treasure

Spying occurs most often in exchange for a monetary payment or some other tangible benefit to the spy, such as medical care or help with practical personal problems. It is the essential lubricant of this clandestine form of commerce. If the truth be known, most intelligence services prefer it that way. They consider it a fee for services rendered, without the complications of faith in a given system or ideology. It is less messy.

Money was critical in the recruitment of Aldrich Ames by the Soviets in 1985. Ames was a thirty-year CIA Soviet Affairs operations officer whose career had topped out at midlevel. He believed he was undervalued by his management and ought to have been promoted to a senior position long before. Then he faced a financial dilemma in the spring of 1985. He had just

returned from an undistinguished overseas assignment in Mexico City, where his long-term problem with alcohol abuse had
resurfaced and made his efforts to cultivate and recruit Soviets
impossible. In addition, he had determined to divorce his wife,
from whom he had separated before undertaking his Mexico
City assignment, and marry Rosario Descazes Dupuy, an attractive Colombian diplomat whom he had befriended in Mexico. To do this he needed a major cash infusion to pay off debt
and fund the alimony he would have to pay in the divorce. He
also saw Rosario as a person of expensive tastes whose lavish
spending habits he would have to support in the future.

Ames's superiors regarded him as an experienced Soviet
operations officer who could speak Russian, write briefing
memos, and handle cases involving recruited Soviets, but he
was not a recruiter of new sources and had this persistent
problem of alcohol abuse. Nonetheless, although he had been
reprimanded and sent to the medics by his chain of command
for his drunken behavior and poor ops performance in Mexico City, he found a more sensitive and important job await-
ing him on his return to Washington, through the old-boy
network and the proclivity of his Mexico City management
to "pass the trash." Latin America wanted no more of him,
but a former superior in New York asked him to take the Soviet counterintelligence slot in the operations directorate, and
none of his drunken escapades in Mexico City surfaced to
knock him out of the running.

No job could have provided him more access to counterintelligence information of enormous value to the Soviets. He
was in position to report on all cases of CIA and FBI spies

then reporting on the Soviets, a fantastic mother lode of coun-terintelligence to the KGB and USSR.

Ames was a volunteer to Soviet intelligence in order to gain enough money to position himself for the future with his new wife. If he had any ideological reasons for his actions they were secondary. He had participated in a number of boozy lunches with an intelligent Russian TASS correspondent when he was stationed in New York in the 1970s, and they talked about the waste and futility of the competition between the two superpowers. It might therefore have been concluded by Soviet intelligence that Ames had lost the faith and was ripe for recruitment. Nonetheless, it was Ames who took the initial step toward the Soviets, and he did it to earn $50,000 for the names of several Soviet officials spying for the United States that Ames believed the Soviets already had a line on. This was in April 1985, and Ames claims that this was the extent of his commitment to the Soviets at that time.

Viktor Cherkashin states in his autobiography that he was successful in moving Ames from the one-time betrayal of allegedly already compromised Soviet cases for $50,000 to "the big dump" in June 1985, when Ames revealed the names of all the Soviet agents working for the United States for an at that moment unnegotiated sum of money.[1] In other words, Ames decided to betray every secret about Soviet operations of which he was aware from one of the most sensitive positions in U.S. intelligence on the basis of Cherkashin's representation that he had crossed the Rubicon with his April transaction. He might as well disgorge everything he knew and profit handsomely from it, because he could never be sure that a U.S. mole in Soviet intelligence would not inform the CIA that the KGB had acquired a new penetration of American intelligence. The only way Ames could protect himself from such a contingency, Cherkashin claims he argued, was to denounce every U.S. operation against the Soviets. In this genuine wilderness of mirrors, it was a question of betraying a potential informant before he betrayed you.

I do not know whether or not to credit Cherkashin's explanation of Ames's decision to go beyond his April revelations for what turned out to be the payment of a $1.7 million bonanza for the biggest disclosure of counterintelligence information to the Soviets during the cold war. To further complicate the picture, Cherkashin's account could be a mischievous ploy to divert attention from an as yet undiscovered additional Soviet/Russian penetration of U.S. intelligence. Nevertheless, there are echoes of Cherkashin's explanation in what Ames told his FBI inquisitors after his arrest in 1994, and in what he told the CIA inspector general's investigators subsequently.

In any event, the payment to Ames was the biggest commitment of money for espionage by the Soviets during this period. The KGB's contemporaneous payments to the FBI's Robert P. Hanssen, while smaller in total amount, bought equally damaging U.S. secrets.

Hanssen was a different kind of volunteer to Soviet intelligence than Aldrich Ames. As Hanssen saw it, he needed money to top up a modest FBI salary and cost-of-living allowance in order to educate his five children at conservative Catholic schools, but his motivation to spy for the Soviets was more than monetary. Hanssen was a complex character, very gifted in information technology matters, but never one of the boys at the bureau. He was never a street agent as Ames was never a spy recruiter, and he deeply resented that fact. In the lonely world he inhabited, he may have convinced himself that he could succeed in spying for the Soviets; get the money he needed to permit his family to live at the level he wanted for them; teach his colleagues at the bureau that they were wrong to undervalue him, and still maintain his arch conservative outlook on life.[2] For these reasons, Robert Hanssen's spying is sui generis.

Pyotr Popov, who volunteered to U.S. intelligence in 1958 by leaving a note in an official U.S. vehicle in Vienna, was a more typical spy for hire. He claimed he needed funds to get his Serbian girlfriend an abortion, and he was willing to bring out as many secrets about Soviet military intelligence as he could carry to earn it. He hated the Soviet system for what it had done to his peasant family in the Ukraine during the period of Stalinist collectivization in the 1930s, but he might never have been driven to espionage but for a desperate need for funds to take care of a pressing personal problem.

Not to be overlooked among the tools available to spy recruiters are nonmonetary forms of reward. On many occasions in the Middle East and in locations where medical care is not up to Western standards, the offer of a life-saving or life-changing medical procedure is more valuable than cash to a potential spy or a family member. In former senior operations officer Dewey Clarridge's account of his life in the CIA, he noted that he was able to offer a potential Polish recruit help in terminating his wife's pregnancy so that they could remain abroad, which they strenuously wished to do.[3] Irina Adamsky aborted naturally, but Clarridge's offer helped him boost an agent relationship with her husband because of his gratitude for an offer of help at a critical time. Agent recruitment in times of personal distress takes on all manner of forms if the West is prepared to use its natural advantages.

Fortunately, these advantages remain available in confronting the challenge of Islamist terrorism. The advertisement of immense monetary rewards has not yet been successful in leading to the capture of Osama bin Laden, but it brought in Saddam Hussein and several prominent Al Qaeda operatives. In addition, this is an area where the United States, working through surrogates or principal agents, can be very effective. It may not be possible for an American case officer to get close to an inviting terrorist target individual, but a cooperating Pakistani or Jordanian intelligence officer might and can relay the offer of U.S. monetary or material assistance, or do it in his own name. There are myriad ways to skin this cat. The critical thing to remember is that even in the face of overwhelming counterpressure—of control in the case of Stalin's police state, and anti-Western dogma in areas of the Middle East—there is always an opportunity for the spy runner to gain an advantage, created by human need or greed. Ames, Hanssen, and Popov prove this.

Sometimes money or material assistance does not help, and may even hinder an agent recruitment. It may be that an act of human friendship comes to mean more between individuals than filthy lucre. There was something in the relationship between Oleg Penkovsky and U.S. Army colonel Charles MacLean Peeke in Turkey in the mid-1950s, when both were serving as their respective country's military attachés, that awoke Penkovsky's respect and kindled his determination to volunteer for the United States. Just because U.S. intelligence has the capacity in most instances to play the money card does not mean that it is appropriate or necessary to do so.

In addition, one must analyze the strange case of John Walker Lindh, who studied Arabic and Islam in northern California before embarking on an odyssey to the Middle East in 2000. It terminated in a Taliban training camp, where he took up arms against the Northern Alliance, and eventually the United States. Lindh was captured by Northern Alliance and U.S. soldiers on the same day and in the same area that CIA officer Johnny Spann was killed in a firefight. Lindh was imprisoned and returned to the United States, and tried and convicted of aiding an enemy of the United States. Apparently, just because of the sincerity of his Islamist views, he had been accepted by the Taliban, and allegedly had met Osama bin Laden on two occasions. If it was possible for Lindh to walk into the inner sanctum of Osama's Taliban operation by taking an anti-American, Islamist stance, it ought to have been open to the German security police to try to attend Mohamed Atta's Hamburg mosque with an eye to cracking his cell. Likewise, the FBI is doubtless seeking to infiltrate radical mosques in the United States akin to the one in Jersey City where Sheikh Omar Abdul-Rahman held forth in the mid-1990s. Although this danger is probably self-evident to radical jihadists, it is often surprising how far persistent informants can get if they are prepared to talk the talk and assert acceptable bona fides. In Lindh's case it was merely a passionate belief in Islamist doctrine. But you have to be prepared to speak the language and understand the milieu.

Finally, there is the case of Harold Nicholson, uncovered shortly after Aldrich Ames's arrest in 1994. Nicholson, an experienced midlevel CIA operations officer, needed money to pay alimony to his ex-spouse in Oregon, and rather than approach his CIA colleagues, he asked for help from his Russian friends, who were ostensibly his operational targets. They, of course, demanded some quid pro quo for their assistance, and he forked over the intelligence. The question immediately arose as to why Nicholson felt closer to his Soviet intelligence friends than his own countrymen when it came to dealing with one of life's more difficult but fairly normal crises. After all, the CIA has mechanisms to help its officers who fall into this kind of financial bind. The answers were never clear. He may have been ashamed of his divorce and the rupture it brought to a family with young children, and he wanted to handle the costs of it out of the office. Or, more likely, being fairly conventional himself, he may have believed that his financial need would unfairly crimp an intelligence career that had demonstrated great promise up to the point of his betrayal. Perhaps he believed he would be revealing a lack of judgment and a character deficiency that in his strait-laced view of the world his superiors might hold against him. In any event, strange things occur in this closeted world of espionage, and money or material reward is often at the heart of it.

Chapter Four

Revenge and Score Settling

Ideological commitment and a need for money are two more or less affirmative reasons for becoming a spy. Less admirable in this look at the seven principal motivations for espionage is a desire for revenge, or to settle a long-term grievance.

Robert P. Hanssen, the FBI spy for the Soviets, wanted to show his loyal wife (and the memory of his father) that he could amount to something, and provide adequately for his family, or so his psychiatrist deduced from long interviews in jail.[1] He also wanted to get back at those in the FBI who called him "Dr. Doom" behind his back, and never let him into the inner circle of the bureau's infamous locker room culture. Thus Hanssen, a conservative Catholic who attended an Opus Dei church with then-director of the FBI Louis Freeh, betrayed to the Soviets every secret that came across his desk during a twenty-year, on-again-off-again career as a Soviet spy. His treachery took place even though he never shared Soviet values or a communist ideology; he never demanded payment from the Soviets commensurate with the value of the information he transferred. Although they were nearly contemporaneous in their spying, Hanssen was never paid what Ames got from the Soviets. Why? In a secret world where the opportunities to settle scores or gain revenge on a system that undervalues the case officer are limited, betraying the organization's secrets by becoming a spy offers a way. It is remarkable how many successful United States and Soviet spy cases during the cold war included the spy attempting to teach his own government or spy service a lesson for having passed over or failed to recognize his superior qualities.

There are garden variety examples, like CIA operations center employee William Kampiles, who stole a valuable technical manual on overhead spy satellite technology in 1977 and sold it to the Soviets. He had no grand political motive for his betrayal, nor did he receive a big payment for his prize. He was just a journeyman spy who was bitter that his CIA career had not taken off, so he betrayed its trust by selling state-of-the-art spy technology for a pittance.

Edward Lee Howard's case was deemed by Director of Central Intelligence (DCI) William J. Casey to have been handled so egregiously that it led to a policy reversal on how disgruntled employees are handled. Howard was a new CIA operations trainee in the early 1980s, whose record was free of any prior involvement in espionage, so he was selected for a sensitive posting to Moscow, because it was believed that the KGB had not yet identified him. He was consequently briefed on a range of sensitive operations being run out of Moscow and adjoining countries. However, it surfaced in a final polygraph screening prior to his departure for Moscow that Howard had been and might still be a drug and alcohol abuser and a petty thief. The CIA canceled his assignment and summarily fired him. Disgruntled at the way he had been treated, Howard volunteered his services to the Soviet Embassy in Washington and engineered a James Bond–like escape from FBI surveillance, departing the country shortly thereafter. He contributed substantially to KGB knowledge of U.S. intelligence operations in Moscow, overlapping some of the data Ames would later provide. He died suddenly in 2002 in Russia, hitting his head in a nasty fall down stairs.

Because the brusque manner of Howard's dismissal appeared to prompt his decision to defect to the Soviets, it became CIA policy thereafter to let misfits down more lightly. Operations officers like Howard, who for one reason or another did not measure up, are still ushered to the door, but not thrown out abruptly. They are given tide-me-over contracts until they can secure other work, and are briefed on their legal responsibility to remain silent on matters they have learned on the inside. It can be argued, however, that this more humane approach to dismissal creates problems of its own. Ames, for example, was assigned to an analytical post in the counternarcotics center when suspicion began to jell in 1993 that he was a Soviet agent. Yet he was still able to provide his Soviet control with lots of good intelligence gleaned from clever use of his office personal computer, and from hanging out with his former Soviet ops colleagues, who loved to gossip about ongoing cases despite the injunction on "need to know." Discharging dishonest or disloyal spies is not easy, and since there is no "turkey farm" that they can be shipped off to—there are no jobs in the back room or on the loading dock for trained spy handlers in which they could be employed safely out of earshot of classified information—it makes the decision to terminate a knowledgeable employee who will not be prosecuted for his inadequacies a tough one. It is not free from risk.

Revenge and score settling were not all on the U.S. side during the cold war. As mentioned above, Pyotr Popov was not deterred in his decision to betray his Soviet military intelligence comrades in Vienna by any love for the Soviet leadership. He had seen his family liquidated in part, and their Ukrainian landholdings collectivized by order of the Supreme Soviet, so he had no use for Stalin's secret police.

Oleg Penkovsky believed that he would never be promoted to field rank in Soviet military intelligence because his father had fought for the White Russians against the Bolsheviks in the 1920s. Despite the fact that he had amassed a fine record during the "great patriotic war," and that he had friends in high places, he never believed that the top job would be open to him because of this blot on his family past. This clearly contributed to his decision to spy for the British and Americans.

What is important about many of these cold war cases of espionage for revenge is that they involve insiders who make their decision to betray knowing to whom they wish to convey their basket of secrets and how they want to do it. In the cases of Ames and Hanssen they knew they wanted to be dealing with their storied opposite number Viktor Cherkashin, because of his experience, competence, and well-established reputation for safeguarding his agents. For example, Cherkashin carried details from Ames's debriefings in person from the Soviet Embassy in Washington, where he was serving, to Moscow rather than trust the KGB's encrypted electronic transmissions.

That situation will likely not hold true in the future. During 1985, the "year of the spy" (so labeled by the media because of the number of espionage cases that came to light during that year, such as the Walker spy ring in the U.S. Navy), it was a fair comment to talk about "spy wars." This term referred to Western intelligence agencies doing battle with the KGB to suborn each other's operatives to achieve penetrations, primarily for counterintelligence reasons. The Walker spy ring was a family operation that stole the Navy's nuclear submarine secrets over nearly a ten-year time span.

This is not how the game is likely to unfold with Islamist terrorism, the West's priority intelligence concern now. The CIA is not working eyeball to eyeball, elbow to elbow against Al Qaeda's intelligence officers, nor are the Pakistanis or the Jordanians. As far as one can make out, our knowledge about who makes the operational decisions and how they are made in choosing Western targets for attack is nonexistent. This means the entire proposition of penetrating Al Qaeda by exploiting individual grievances or frustrations is much more complex. The *9/11 Commission Report* makes that abundantly clear. It notes that Mohamed Atta, the Egyptian ringleader of the 9/11 hijackers, experienced some difficulty in keeping all of his eighteen colleagues in line during the run-up to the infamous day of attack. Several wanted to depart the United States without any assurance that they would be able to return for the event, in order to take care of personal business. If the CIA or FBI had been able to identify or understand the past histories and personal rivalries roiling this group, it might have succeeded in pulling one or two of them off during their two-year preparations.

Because there is no Al Qaeda embassy or cultural mission in Washington, London, or Karachi, we do not even see or know against whom we are operating for the most part. What Western intelligence services are up against is more akin to detective or basic police work. We shall have to identify Islamist cells and peel back the onion one layer of skin at a time to identify targets, as the French army did in Algiers in the 1950s.

It is a far more challenging puzzle than looking at a cadre of Soviet or Chinese officials and trying to determine who are the intelligence officers, and then assessing their vulnerabilities. For the most part, we are still in the position of trying to figure out who and where the bad guys are. This was made abundantly clear in a statement in August 2005 by the new director of the NSA, Lieutenant General Keith B. Alexander, who noted that his current mission is literally akin to searching for a needle in a haystack. NSA, which operates America's sigint, is assigned to capture, record, decrypt if necessary, and analyze millions and millions of cell phone calls and e-mail messages worldwide. They do this in order to identify in a timely manner the handful of messages that might signal preparations for a terrorist attack. It is an impossible job, made even more so by the limited number of Arabic-speaking analysts currently employed by NSA.

This, of course, raises the entire issue of technological boosts to intelligence gathering and analysis. With physical access to human spies becoming more difficult, the West must again count on what made it successful during the era of cold war espionage—sophisticated technology. The twenty-first century's equivalent of the development of spy satellites must be the West's mastery of Internet technology, in order to trace international money flows among terrorist organizations and the daily correspondence between terrorist Web sites and cells planning attacks. It appears, for example, that much of the tactical communication between individual members of terrorist cells in the Middle East and their chain of command takes place openly over the Internet, through the medium of Arabic-language terrorist Web sites that are constantly changing. NSA and others will have to find ways to canvass these Web sites and mine the data being shared. And it will not be able to do this alone. Such a monumental task will have to be undertaken with help from the West's friends in the region, who are closer to the scene, and who understand the vernacular and the import of indirect references that denote hostile intent or planning. The U.S. intelligence community used bureaucratese to describe this kind of situation during the cold war era, when it knew what it had to do and where to go to solve an intelligence problem but had not yet worked out all the technical steps to do so. It would describe the problem as "technology forcing." In other words, the problem itself would create the pressure and the path to devise a technical solution, just as the impenetrability of the USSR brought on the overhead reconnaissance technology, first by U-2 aircraft and eventually by satellite, that allowed us to understand the Soviet missile program. We see such a need today in countless ways. And it gives the lie to those who declare that all one has to do is get more spy runners on the Arab street. Their presence will be useless unless their efforts are enhanced by the fruits of Internet-derived tactical intelligence on whom they are looking for and what must be protected.

Chapter Five

Sex, Intimidation, and Blackmail

By now the reader has concluded that none of the principal motivations for espionage so far enumerated exists in an isolated state. A spy may betray his country for both ideological *and* monetary reasons, but also to wreak revenge on a system that has not recognized and employed his talents to the fullest. The following three reasons to spy are similarly intertwined. An agent may be entrapped through a sexual ploy that he is determined not be revealed to his employer. The spy may not be ideologically drawn to the spymaster's cause but is afraid to confront his situation and allows himself to be blackmailed or intimidated by the spymaster. Finally, there may be an element of ethnic or religious solidarity in the spy's affirmative response to the spymaster's pitch. We shall consider these three aspects of espionage consecutively.

Neither the British nor the American intelligence services made much use of sexual entrapment during the cold war. This was in all likelihood a decision not made for reasons of scruple, but rather because it didn't work. Soviets and central Europeans were used to a much more rough-and-tumble lifestyle than their Western counterparts and a secretly photographed liaison with a luscious blonde not your wife or with a same-sex partner would not lead to a betrayal of state secrets in most instances.

When the shoe was on the other foot, however, the Soviet intelligence services profited handsomely from a tradition of launching "swallows" at lonely Western officials, trapped in tightly controlled if drab circumstances behind the Iron Curtain. Swallows were well-trained female Soviet intelligence officers schooled in all the arts of Western allurement, like Tatiana Romanova in Ian Fleming's *From Russia with Love*. Their job was to seduce the unwary or oversexed Westerner, and the KGB would be waiting behind the arras to photograph the liaison, unbeknownst to the hapless victim. The pictures would then be used to get the Western diplomat to "cooperate" with his Soviet hosts or face exposure to his embassy.

Felix Bloch was an Austrian-born American diplomat who returned to the city of his birth, Vienna, in 1980 as a high-ranking U.S. embassy officer. Among the first things he proceeded to do upon arrival was arrange a weekly tryst with a local prostitute who specialized in sadomasochistic sex. According to newspaper accounts, Bloch paid his whip-wielding partner the large sum of $250 per week for his visits, or more than $10,000 a year, for seven years. Soviet intelligence must have gotten wind of this affair, either through photographs taken of the liaison, or by offering to help Bloch defray its expenses, because they soon recruited him and put him in touch with an "illegal" agent of theirs named Reino Gikman.[1] The FBI believed Gikman was a courier of documents between Bloch and the KGB for nearly ten years. Unfortunately, the Soviet spy in the FBI, Robert Hanssen, tipped the Soviets off to FBI suspicions about Bloch, and the KGB quickly dropped contact with him. Although Bloch was later forced out of the State Department, the FBI never had an opportunity to prove his espionage in court because of the Hanssen tip-off. This is a classic case where an operative's vulnerability to sexual entrapment provided the opening for blackmail and cooperation by intimidation.

The sad story of Marine security guard Clayton J. Lonetree provided another example in 1987. In the Lonetree case, a homesick young Native American security guard first at the U.S. Embassy in Moscow and then Vienna fell prey to the beauty of a Soviet translator in the Moscow embassy. Against all rules, his infatuation led him eventually to a meeting with her "Uncle Sasha," a KGB agent, who, after getting Lonetree to identify CIA personnel in the embassy and provide a floor plan, then proposed that he admit Soviet intelligence officers into the vaulted and restricted areas of the chancery. Happily, Lonetree realized he was in over his head and turned himself in to the CIA chief, and the intrusion never came to pass. But it was a near miss, and it showed the dilemmas of innocent, unprepared, and immature Americans working abroad and the speed with which Soviet intelligence was prepared to exploit such a vulnerability. Once again, the key to Soviet near success in the Lonetree operation was the KGB's complete control of the operational environment within the USSR. There was no way to fully escape the Soviet ability to put attractive young women in the path of alienated, lonely, and inexperienced targets. There were few other outlets.

A similar loneliness or unfulfilled expectation caused U.S. embassy officer Sharon Scranage to become involved with a flamboyant Ghanaian lothario in Accra in 1983. Ms. Scranage was a proud African American who had fallen in love with the African continent as much as her intelligence officer boyfriend Michael Soussoudis, but her actions did nothing to help the CIA's Ghanaian agents who were betrayed by Ms. Scranage to the Ghanaian intelligence service.

Does spying for sex offer any prospect for success against Arabs in the Middle East who have taken up the cause of Islamist fundamentalism? On the surface, the answer would appear to be a quick yes. Sex outside wedlock in Islam is against Koranic scripture. If an Al Qaeda Islamist zealot were entrapped in a sexual liaison with a Western nonbeliever, would that not be a promising basis on which to get him to spill the beans or collaborate against his terrorist buddies?

One would think so, but the evidence of such clumsy efforts at sexual compromise as occurred at Abu Ghraib in 2003 would argue otherwise. There is no evidence that sexual intimidation or humiliation, whether by dressing Arab prisoners in female undergarments or taunting them before female guards, produced any positive intelligence in Abu Ghraib, if that was the purpose behind the intimidation. Perhaps the most promising avenue in using sex as a tool against Islamists might be to try to trap them into failing to respond appropriately to a sexual slur cast at one of their family members, such as loss of virginity.

For the most part, I believe Western intelligence operators are too naïve about the sexual mores of Arab Islamists to use sex as a tool for espionage or intimidation. Abu Ghraib is a clear indicator of that.

Related to spying for sex is the use of blackmail and intimidation as a recruitment tool for spies. And in a vein similar to sex, American and British intelligence have traditionally shied away from using extortion as a tool. As in the opposition to the use of sex, the reluctance is less from moral scruple than for reasons of operational effectiveness. Perhaps we are too conditioned in the West to think that it is far more productive to rely on positive reinforcements like money or ideology to lure someone into treachery than the threat of exposure or intimidation. Maybe we are just not very good at threatening reprisals or blackmail.

Surely the cases mentioned earlier involve the threat of sexual compromise to produce cooperation in acts of espionage. Felix Bloch did not want his foreign service career upended by his taste for kinky sex; likewise Sergeant Lonetree thought too much of his lover, Violetta Sanni, to have her lose her job as translator in the embassy if their affair was exposed. And in Sharon Scranage's case, her lover told her he would abandon her if she ceased to supply him with intelligence information.

Yet there is an element of blackmail and coercion in every spy relationship. Once a spy has crossed the Rubicon and delivered secrets to his handler, he can't go back to the life he had before. He is a traitor and has betrayed his trust. Victor Cherkashin played on this vulnerability in urging Aldrich Ames to make the big dump in June 1985, after he had already sold fifty thousand dollars' worth of secrets in April. According to Cherkashin, he made Ames believe that if he did not bring out all the names of Soviets spying for the Americans, one of them might in time denounce *him*. Likewise, even after confessing to espionage for the Soviets to his priest at his wife Bonny's insistence, and promising to give the wages of his sin to Mother Teresa, Robert Hanssen found himself back in a few years supplying the Soviets with critical information. He told them about the FBI's techniques for shadowing Soviet diplomats in New York and the listening post the United States was building under the new Soviet embassy in Washington. Espionage is a bit like the irreversible bond reputedly forged by the Mafiosi: Once in, you can seldom get out. The act of spying creates an intimidating pressure to continue and to conform.

There is no direct way to make the events reportedly taking place at Abu Ghraib, Guantánamo, and the mysterious secret CIA prisons in Eastern Europe applicable to this discussion of the role of blackmail and intimidation in espionage, but they are relevant. The reported use of water-boarding and other highly coercive techniques to make Khalid Sheikh Mohammed talk aroused concern that the CIA was exceeding the limits permitted in the questioning of terrorist suspects, even though he was allegedly a mastermind of the 9/11 attacks. If the CIA is perceived to not be bound by the U.S. government's own strictures against torture or the use of cruel and inhuman punishment in defiance of customary international law, won't that spill over to their normal espionage activities? Won't potential and existing spies wonder what's in store for them if they get caught crosswise with their spy handler, or a misunderstanding develops about their access or reporting? It sounds far-fetched, but these events never take place in a vacuum. Just as it is known in the world of espionage which services honor their obligations to pay the monies earned by captured or executed spies to their relatives, so it is known how spy services treat and protect their agents.

Fortunately, U.S. intelligence agencies have not been exempted from the McCain Amendment, which became law in December 2005 as part of the Detainee Treatment Act (DTA). This law forbids U.S. personnel in U.S. facilities from using coercive interrogation techniques not set forth in the U.S. Army interrogation manual, which prohibits torture and cruel and inhuman punishment.

The question is still outstanding, however, as to the fate of Khalid Sheikh Mohammed and the thirteen other high-value Al Qaeda prisoners transferred in late 2006 to Guantánamo by President Bush to stand trial for war crimes. These proceedings will take place in conformity with the Military Commissions Act of 2006 that contains explicit provisions embracing the standards of the DTA. The Military Commissions Act states that evidence obtained by torture or coercive interrogations ("cruel, unusual and inhuman treatment") prohibited by Common Article 3 of the Geneva Conventions of

1949 may not be admitted. Since Khalid Sheikh Mohammed and the other transferees were interrogated in CIA custody in secret prisons, and some have reportedly confessed, can these confessions be used against them in their trials before military commissions if they were brought about before passage of the Military Commissions and the Detainee Treatment acts by techniques not prescribed in the Army field manual? This is a tough question that is bound to influence the attitude of friendly cooperating intelligence services in the war on terror, and potential and existing U.S. spies who may wonder what impact these practices will have on their own relationships with U.S. intelligence.

Chapter Six

Spying for Reasons of Friendship or Ethnic or Religious Solidarity

A powerful motivation for spying, and one that is often underappreciated, is simple friendship. As noted earlier, Oleg Penkovsky was drawn to American military attaché Charles MacLean Peeke when they served together in 1955 in Ankara. His admiration for this tall army officer was clearly one of the reasons he volunteered to spy for the West in 1961. He was already beginning to become alienated by the crass favoritism accorded the select *nomenklatura* who buttered up their superiors to gain extra privileges and cushy assignments in the Soviet system. He contrasted this with the perceived professional approach of the Americans who went about their business in a straightforward manner. To be sure,

Penkovsky was already looking for another vessel into which to pour his confidence, having lost faith in his own, but Colonel Peeke gave him someone to look up to as the embodiment of that new value system.

Dewey Clarridge made a similar friend in Polish trade attaché Wladyslaw Adamsky during their service together in Turkey in the 1960s. As he describes Adamsky's development in his autobiography, *A Spy for All Seasons,* Clarridge managed to get Adamsky to surmount the normal barriers of Polish security so that they could meet on social occasions. But it was not until, in an ultimate act of friendship, he offered to provide Irina Adamsky with an abortion pill to terminate an unwanted pregnancy that he was able to recruit Wladyslaw to espionage. In the event, Irina aborted naturally, but Clarridge's offer would have prevented a certain recall to Poland that was against the Adamskys' wishes. Such are the events that turn friendships into something more.

The relationship to one another of the Cambridge Five, who spied for the Soviet Union in the 1930s, involved their membership in a society of aesthetes at the university called "The Apostles" who were sworn never to betray one another. The Apostles became a recruiting ground for the KGB during that time, in that Anthony Blunt and Guy Burgess (to name two leaders of the infamous five) spotted the others, using the society and its rule of silence to first evaluate their commitment to communism, and then captivate them, after some rudimentary tasking was successfully accomplished. Michael Straight, the American Apostle, never came forward to denounce Burgess and MacLean when he encountered them in Washington during the early cold war period because of the Apostles' pledge not to rat on a brother member. He warned Burgess that he would break his vow unless Burgess departed U.S. shores, which he subsequently did, but Straight eventually overcame his student pledge in denouncing Blunt in 1963.

Finally, unilateral recruitments when they occur between intelligence officers in official contact or liaison with one another appear to be based at least in part on friendship. When an American intelligence officer leans over a glass of whiskey and asks his opposite number in a European service to hand over a particular report that had hitherto been embargoed to the United States, he is asking for a favor that in time might ripen into a unilateral recruitment to spy for the United States. Where the United States has been in a strong position to materially aid the career as well as the personal wherewithal of such an official, the temptation to step over the line and accept spy tasking has been strong.

In the global war on terror, such as it is, in which the Bush administration has been engaged since 9/11, personnel in friendly intelligence services in the Middle East are certain to have become particular targets for development and then recruitment. Middle Eastern intelligence services with close ties to their populations and cultures have a bottomless appetite for Western technological and material assistance. Friendships are formed in the pursuit of compatible targets, which ripen into unilateral recruitments of senior personnel, when the United States is willing to share its resources and technology to make the recruited official look good in the performance of his duties. As a consequence, we have reached important unilateral understandings with some intelligence and political chiefs in the region as a result of our willingness to spread our good fortune around, rather than in the customary manner of fees for services rendered.

One of the strongest motivations for spying, and one with obvious relevance today, is a common ethnic, cultural, or religious tie between a spy and the country or entity that recruits him. The most gripping case in American annals is that of Jonathan Pollard, who was arrested in 1985 for spying for Israel. Pollard was an American Jew working in U.S. Naval Intelligence, who passed thousands of sensitive documents to Israel out of apparent concern for that country's well-being. Although Pollard had denied that he spied for Israel because *he* is a Jew, his sympathy for the Israeli cause and his view of his "ethnic obligation" to help Israel belie his protestations. He appears to have suffered some anti-Semitism growing up in South Bend, Indiana, as part of a small minority in a tough neighborhood that may have accentuated his attachment to his Jewish identity. In any event, he developed a strong admiration for the state of Israel from an early age, even attempting to volunteer for military service in Israel while still an undergraduate at Stanford during the Yom Kippur War in 1973. In short, service to Israel became an obsession, and he volunteered to spy for the Israeli intelligence service, passing quantities of classified information on a whole range of delicate subjects to his Israeli spymaster, not just secrets bearing on issues related to the state of Israel. Pollard was caught, tried, and found guilty of spying for Israel, and is now being held in life imprisonment. Periodically, the government of Israel petitions the U.S. president to release Pollard, arguing that he has paid his debt for the crime of espionage between allies. Indeed, Pollard was nearly used as a bargaining chip in negotiations between Israel and the PLO in 2000 by President Clinton, but DCI George Tenet put his foot down and threatened to resign over the issue. This is one of the clearest instances of espionage for ethnic and religious reasons.

The particularly close ties that bind American Jews to Israel are paralleled to some degree in the relationship between some Chinese Americans and the People's Republic of China (PRC), at least in the eyes of the Chinese government. Two recent cases stand out, but they still retain an aura of mystery.

Larry Wu-Tai Chin, an intelligence officer in the CIA's Foreign Broadcast Information Service, sold secrets to China for more than thirty years, from 1952 until his arrest in 1985. Although the U.S. government based its legal prosecution of Chin on the theory that he did it for the money ($140,000 was proven to have changed hands, but maybe as much as a million dollars was paid Chin over the length of his service to China), there are indicators from his statements at trial that ethnic sympathy for China also played a large part in his treachery. To be sure, Chin welcomed the money, because he liked to gamble and he speculated on real estate, but the U.S. attorney who prosecuted him declared at trial, "The man's [Chin's] mind and his heart have been in China."[1] He wanted to speed not only the rapprochement between China and the United States but between the peoples of the two countries.

It would appear that China believes that there *are* particular reasons why Chinese Americans are open to a recruitment pitch to spy. Perhaps it boils down to a belief that Chinese everywhere take ethnic pride at seeing China reclaim the position of cultural and economic preeminence that it once enjoyed. Nonetheless, there is little question that Chinese intelligence aggressively pursues this hoped-for feeling of ethnic solidarity in its approach to Chinese Americans.

That brings us to the peculiar case of Wen Ho Lee, a U.S. scientist of Chinese ethnicity, born in Taiwan, who worked on sensitive nuclear matters for many years at the Los Alamos National Laboratory in New Mexico. In 1999, Lee was accused of supplying sensitive nuclear bomb technology to agents of China. The accusation arose from a sensitive intelligence community report claiming that China had acquired the specifications for a newly designed nuclear weapon that was being developed at Los Alamos. This intelligence report followed a lengthy series of hearings on Capitol Hill on China's practice of inviting and sending delegations of armaments experts and scientists to and from the United States in an effort to increase its armaments expertise. The hearings created a heightened sensitivity in Washington to the manner in which China appeared to be exploiting enhanced contacts between U.S. and Chinese scientists to gather sophisticated technical information on advanced U.S. weapons projects. When it became publicized that in fact U.S. intelligence believed that China had stolen the design of the new nuclear bomb, the FBI was under enormous pressure to determine how and who might have turned over the information. Lee was singled out because he and his wife had had continuous and intimate social contact over a number of years with Chinese scientists visiting the Los Alamos labs, and he had access to the nuclear bomb specifications that the U.S. government believed China now possessed. In the course of investigating Lee's work station, U.S. government agents discovered that he had downloaded ten very sensitive computer tapes of classified weapons material and that the tapes were missing.

Although Lee denied having taken the tapes, they were under his control and the FBI searched extensively for them, even bulldozing a dump in the area to see if they had been discarded there. The missing tapes were never recovered, and the United States was unable to prove that Wen Ho Lee was a spy for China. Lee pled guilty to one count of mishandling classified material and subsequently sued the United States for discrimination and won.

Interestingly enough, the Chinese predilection to approach Americans of Chinese ethnicity first when looking for help in gathering U.S. secrets became tied up with official U.S. aversion to racial profiling in seeking out those with hostile intent toward U.S. policy. When the U.S. Senate looked at the botched prosecution of the Wen Ho Lee case, it felt compelled to draw some interesting conclusions regarding China's preference for approaching Chinese Americans for intelligence-gathering purposes: "To say that the United States Government is cognizant of the fact that the PRC prefers to target individuals for elicitation based on their ethnicity is completely different from saying that an individual would be more likely to engage in espionage because he or she is a member of a particular ethnic group."[2] Fair enough, as a necessary paean to political correctness on the explosive issue of racial profiling, but it really doesn't answer the question. There must have been some success in recruiting Chinese Americans behind China's continual use of the stratagem.

Actually, if there was any racial profiling in the Wen Ho Lee case it was by China, which had duly noted that Lee often felt like a fish out of water socially in the United States, and that he jumped at opportunities to join or host delegations involved in Chinese cultural exchanges. They simply took advantage of his overweening interest in contacts with Chinese scientists.

Finally, there is the case of Ana Belen Montes, who was arrested nine days after 9/11, for spying for Cuba. She had apparently found herself for many years in substantial disagreement with the United States's continuing confrontational policy toward Cuba, and cooperated with Cuban intelligence in keeping Castro's government informed of the twists and turns in U.S. policy in this regard. She especially warned Cuba of any U.S. preparations to act with hostility toward the island. Ms. Montes was of Puerto Rican descent, and at the age of forty-four, a top analyst at the Defense Intelligence Agency (DIA) and the Pentagon's leading expert on Cuba. She had coauthored a widely noted 1998 Defense Department report that opined that Cuba no longer posed a significant military threat to the United States.

What made Montes's betrayal so intriguing, aside from

her high rank and authoritative voice on Cuban matters in the U.S. government, was that she appeared to have been a member of a very patriotic American family. Her sister, a translator for the FBI, helped take down a Cuban spy network in south Florida in 2001. Her brother works for the FBI in the Atlanta area, and her father retired in 1995 from the U.S. Army as a colonel, having been an Army doctor for most of his career. Wherever the seeds of Montes's disaffection came from, it was not from the Montes household. Yet her family was conscious and proud of its Hispanic heritage, and that may have been the wellspring of her attitude toward Cuba. According to Ms. Montes's statements at the time of her trial in October 2002, she appeared to resent the United States's hostile attitude toward Cuba, and she expressed a desire to see the United States develop a more tolerant attitude toward its near neighbor. There is also some evidence that Ms. Montes was a Puerto Rican nationalist who favored Puerto Rican independence. A sympathetic attitude toward a Hispanic neighbor may have morphed into a willingness to spy for Cuba in this proud Latina.

What relevance do the factors of ethnic and religious solidarity as the bases for recruitment to espionage have in the current period? Clearly, the attitude of the Chinese toward the vulnerability of Chinese Americans to an appeal to a common heritage remains an issue. What does that say about the vulnerability of Arab Americans or Muslim Americans to appeals for Islamic solidarity against Westerners in Iraq? This is a question much speculated about by the FBI and homeland security officials, considering the large Muslim

American population living in southeastern Michigan and on the West Coast. For example, in the aftermath of 9/11, the bureau was instructed to round up members of the American Muslim community in the Detroit area in search of undocumented aliens or Arabs who had overstayed their visas. Based on their long-term ties to the community, the FBI performed this task with the cooperation of community leaders, taking care not to be accusatory or overly aggressive. Other post-9/11 roundups were not handled with the same sensitivity, but the American Muslim community has worked hard to publicize the successes as well as the slipups. It made a big difference that President Bush invited an imam to the memorial ceremony at the Washington National Cathedral several days after 9/11. That invitation was intended to send the signal that America's quarrel was with Al Qaeda and the jihadists, not Islam.

In summary, thus far it appears likely that Muslim Americans live and work in this country for the same reasons that most of the rest of us former immigrants do: To provide better lives for their families in the United States and, in the case of immigrants from the Middle East, to get away from the conflicts and limited opportunities they had known in their homelands.

There have been few publicized stories of Al Qaeda attempts at recruitment of Americans beyond Jose Padilla and John Walker Lindh and the Binghamton Muslims, who were all volunteers. But the impact has been far greater in a counterintelligence sense. There appears to be an underlying mistrust of Muslim Americans or Arab Americans in the national security area. This manifests itself in the inability of many patriotic members of these groups to get security clearances when they offer their services to the U.S. government for sensitive antiterrorist assignments, such as translating Internet and other communications from Middle Eastern languages into English. To me this is shortsighted and a return to the attitude that enabled the United States to intern Japanese Americans during World War II. Apparently, many of these clearances are failing because some of the Muslim Americans still have close relatives living in Middle Eastern hot spots. While one must be sensitive to the possibility of blackmail or family pressure, if the candidate has a clean record as an American citizen, the assumption should be made in favor of that citizenship, and he or she should be given the opportunity to serve until circumstances prove otherwise. From all indications about the extraordinary delay encountered in the translation of intercepted messages by NSA and the FBI, there is a serious need for native speakers of Middle Eastern languages. They are also needed as case officers in Arabic-speaking countries. A recent shocking statistic along these lines is contained in the report of the Iraq Study Group (2006) that in the one thousand–person U.S. Embassy in Baghdad there are but six fluent Arabic speakers. Happily, there are signs that the new leadership of the intelligence community understands the problem of a lack of homegrown Muslim Americans in its ranks. The new director of national intelligence, Vice Admiral John M. "Mike" McConnell, has stated that the hiring of qualified first- and second-generation Muslim Americans will be one of his top priorities.

A hostile, suspicious attitude toward the region and toward

Islam generally is a product of fear and our own cultural ignorance. We will have to recruit extensively from the Muslim American community for intelligence officers as well as translators if we are to be successful in dealing with the Al Qaeda threat.

Apart from the Muslim American community, the 9/11 Commission reported that only *six* American students majored in Arabic studies in 2002. *The New York Times* noted six months after the publication of the *9/11 Commission Report* that the figure for Arabic studies majors in 2003 was twenty-two. The United States will not be able to cultivate moderates, much less operate effectively against terrorists in the Middle East, if our language capacities and cultural understanding are so limited. It will be hard enough to find ways to merely develop contact with Muslims who might have access to terrorist targets, but if we cannot speak to them or understand them when we get there, the job will be almost impossible.

In the wake of the *9/11 Commission Report,* and upon the urging of the president, the Congress has passed legislation to encourage training in difficult languages, but there is some question whether sufficient resources have yet been devoted to this enormous task. Many in the intelligence community, the military, and the foreign service believe that we should embark upon a Marshall Plan in the United States to encourage training in difficult languages such as Arabic, Farsi, Pashto, Dari, Chinese, and Japanese. We did it in the era that followed the Soviet launch of the satellite *Sputnik* by passing the National Defense Education Act (NDEA, 1958) to fund the improvement of math and physics departments in universities around the nation, but also in foreign area studies and the study of hard languages. It was considered important to America's national security in the late fifties, and it is no less so today. The NDEA is still on the books but is hopelessly underfunded. The point is that the United States cannot rely just on the call of patriotism to draw students into the difficult study of hard languages. We need to accomplish it the old-fashioned American way: We need to stimulate performance by awarding bountiful stipends, if students are willing to commit to study Arabic to a level of conversational fluency, followed by a five-year hitch in the CIA, FBI, or NSA. It has to be made a patriotic national priority, with the government promoting it to generate excitement among students as was done with President Kennedy's Peace Corps.

Chapter Seven

The Spy Game for the Sake of the Game

There were many instances during the cold war and before when the only way to account for the motivation of a spy or spy runner, or to explain his extraordinary actions in pursuit of a mission, was that he loved the profession for its own sake. Of nobody was this truer than Allen W. Dulles, diplomat and intelligence officer during World War I in Vienna and Bern. By his own account, he had an opportunity to meet V. I. Lenin in Bern in 1917, prior to the latter's return to Moscow in a sealed train, but passed it up for a tennis game. After a successful career between the wars working as a New York lawyer in international finance, he joined General William J. "Wild Bill" Donovan's Office of Strategic Services (OSS) in 1942, and was sent back to be chief in Bern. There, as a quasiovert operative, he performed brilliantly, opening his doors, in his own words, to "purveyors of information, volunteers, and adventurers of every sort, professional and amateur spies, good and bad."[1]

Dulles made and maintained contact with Hitler assassination plotters and a spy who reported on the Nazi V-1 and V-2 rocket projects. By far his most important source, however, was Fritz Kolbe, code-named George Wood, who, after being thrown out of the British military attaché's office in Bern in 1943 as a provocateur, found his way to Dulles. Kolbe was special assistant to a top Nazi diplomat entrusted with the most important missions involving the Nazi military high command. So from 1943 until the end of the war against Germany, this forty-three-year-old spy provided Dulles and the Americans with voluminous documents containing the diplomatic and military correspondence of the leaders of the Third Reich. The documents revealed Hitler's thinking as the war progressed and the fortunes of war changed. Dulles's espionage tradecraft was also taxed to the limit as to how to get the intelligence to the Washington analysts in timely fashion. With Nazi diplomatic cables being carried to him in reams, Dulles sent the sexiest material forward from Geneva to Lyon in a secret compartment on a train, where they were picked up and transported by bicycle to Marseilles, for Corsican smugglers to fly them to Corsica, whence they could be flown to Washington, D.C. In early 1944, Kolbe's intelligence information was so timely on Nazi rocket construction sites and assassination plotting against Hitler that it ended up on President Roosevelt's desk.

With such an exciting wartime experience, it is no wonder

Allen Dulles found it difficult to return to the routine practice of law after the OSS was disbanded in 1945. He believed fervently in the need for a U.S. civilian intelligence service, and testified to that effect before the Senate Armed Services Committee in April 1947, just prior to passage of the National Security Act of 1947 that created the Central Intelligence Agency and the National Security Council. Although he would not become director of central intelligence for another six years, Dulles's involvement in the early shaping of the CIA's activities in covert action and estimative intelligence was critical. He wrote a book titled *The Craft of Intelligence* (1963), newly republished, that attempted to give spy running a patina of professionalism, but underneath it all for him, it was still the "great game" of Kipling's India. It was important, and it was fun. For the most part Dulles believed in classic espionage operations—spy handlers exploiting human foibles, dependent on the quick wits of the case officer and still slightly amateurish. He had little use for the possibilities of the high-tech espionage that would largely come to dominate intelligence gathering after him.

Sadly, not all the practitioners of the spy game possessed Allen Dulles's sense of duty and patriotism. Aldrich Ames and Robert Hanssen were spies for the Soviet Union and Russia for whom just money and ideology could not alone explain their motivation to betray the United States.

Ames exchanged information on a number of counterintelligence operations that he believed the KGB already knew about for $50,000, in order to pay off some existing debt and alimony so he could marry his new Colombian girlfriend, Rosario Dovvorirs Dupuy, in April 1985. Two months later (with or without the prompting of his handler, Victor Cherkashin), he delivered to the Soviets a list of every U.S. asset reporting to the FBI and CIA on the USSR, a list that contained over twenty names. In addition, he continued to supply the Soviets with the details of ongoing U.S. operations against the USSR and the names of U.S. personnel engaged in them until he was arrested in 1994. He never put a price on this enormous betrayal, but he is believed to have received over $1.7 million. The Soviets acted quickly on Ames's information, executing ten of the compromised spies and perhaps several more. It was the biggest intelligence compromise in CIA history and until the Hanssen betrayal the most damaging.

Aldrich Ames was a bundle of conflicting sentiments. Yes, he needed the money, but his hubris was such that he took no care in the spending of it. He ran up credit card debt of many thousands each month, and pursued a lifestyle clearly far in excess of his government salary. He paid cash for his new house in Arlington, Virginia—and never worried about getting his government accountings in on time. He simply did not believe anybody in the CIA was clever enough to catch him, and this narcissism led him to take foolish risks, such as talking about his operational planning over open telephone lines. He thought he was so good at the game of espionage, and his colleagues were such boobs, that he failed to file contact reports on his meetings with Soviet officials, believing that that might go undetected.

Robert Hanssen was a quite different character. He eschewed the flamboyant lifestyle of Ames and, by his own determination, never made a personal meeting with his Soviet handlers. He needed the money the Soviets paid him to send his children to expensive schools and to upgrade the family's standard of living, but his espionage was not based upon money alone. As with Ames, Hanssen had minimal regard for his FBI colleagues. They ridiculed his dark suits and formal manner, but he considered himself to be a lot smarter than they were, especially on technical matters. And this caused him to take some unnecessary risks. For example, he often visited his own personnel file online to see if anybody suspected him of being a Soviet agent. He even waylaid an official report headed for one of his superiors to check to see if it contained any derogatory information on him. He was quite bored with his State Department assignment, keeping track of foreign diplomats in Washington, and yearned to be back in the espionage spotlight supplying the Soviets with meaningful secrets.

As Cherkashin noted in his autobiography, Hanssen's contribution to Soviet knowledge about U.S. security practices, spy technology, and spy operations hostile to the USSR was far greater than that of Aldrich Ames, although it may have cost fewer agent lives. Hanssen provided positive intelligence information on happenings at the forefront of U.S. efforts against the Soviet Union, not merely agents engaged in the perpetual struggle of spy vs. spy In that sense Hanssen was the most damaging spy for the Soviets against the United States during the cold war. For example, during his time of spying for the Soviets he had identified the ways in which the FBI tracked Soviet spies in New York. He gave away the listening post that had been constructed adjacent to the new Soviet embassy on Mount Alto in Washington, D.C.

All this came from a convinced political and social conservative who remained strongly anticommunist throughout his years of espionage for the Soviet Union. How does one account for these blatant contradictions? Is it all just the money? My reading of Hanssen and the letters he wrote to his spy handlers, which were filed as affidavits in his criminal trial, is that, like Ames, he felt invincible. He did not believe the Russians knew his identity, and he did not think anyone in the bureau was smart enough to trip him up. This overconfidence joined with some of fate's ironies to convince Hanssen that he could always stay one jump ahead of his pursuers. For example, he was the FBI officer chosen to search for the third mole after Edward Lee Howard's and Ames's treachery could not explain all the compromised Soviet cases in 1985 and 1986, and he *was* that mole. I believe he relished the thought. He enjoyed being the one person who did know what was going on—until he became overly burdened with his betrayal and his need to live several lives—and he almost came to relish his capture. "What took you so long?" he reportedly asked his FBI captors.

Thus, one of the qualities the CIA must be looking for in its pursuit of individuals prepared to betray their friends, family, professional associates, and country to spy for us is a relish for the game of espionage itself. More than (or in addition to) money, sex, ideology, friendship, revenge, or ethnic solidarity, a potential spy must be comfortable in the duplicitous role-playing and manipulation of people that spying often demands. Furthermore, he or she must be good at it.

Part Two

America's Spying Competence Today

In the wake of the much publicized intelligence failures that preceded the 9/11 attacks, and the failure to find Iraqi WMD before or after going to war in March 2003, it is commonly known that the competence of the intelligence community today is in question. This part will explore the intelligence community's capacity to meet the challenge of jihadist terrorism in order to supply the intelligence information that will enable President Bush and his successors to prevent or preempt a future 9/11-like terrorist attack.

We should stipulate that preventing future 9/11s is the intelligence community's top priority, although force protection of and intelligence aid to the war fighters in Iraq and Afghanistan are of equal importance. I shall narrow the evaluation even further. Even though Iran, North Korea, and China represent significant targets of U.S. intelligence collection and analysis, the challenge of the war on terror is paramount. Further, although most of the sixteen intelligence community components currently reporting to the director of national intelligence are involved in some way or another in pursuit of the terrorist target, we are primarily interested here in human source espionage that remains the responsibility of the CIA, FBI, and DIA.

The National Security Agency collects signals intelligence that is a very important source of intelligence on terrorist activity. It intercepts cell phone signals and other forms of data transmission.

Specialized bureaus in policy-making government departments, such as the Bureau of Intelligence and Research (INR) in the State Department and components of the Treasury Department (tracking illegal cash flows) and the Energy Department (identifying the uses of high-grade aluminum tubes), also play a major role.

The National Reconnaissance Office and the National Geospatial Intelligence Agency collect and interpret data from the U.S. satellite "eyes in the sky." They usually play a lesser role in the war on terror.

The Defense Intelligence Agency has a humint service, and occasionally gets pulled into intelligence collection against terrorists in a war zone, assisted sometimes by the intelligence elements of the uniformed services. There have been recent public reports that special DOD operatives have helped Ethiopia quash Al Qaeda elements in Somalia by supplying overhead reconnaissance pictures and lethal weapons to Ethiopian fighters.

The Department of Homeland Security is interested in the domestic implications of the intelligence information on terrorism gathered by the CIA and the FBI particularly.

However, in assessing the preparedness and health of the intelligence community's efforts against the United States's priority target, global terrorism, we are most interested in the competence of two agencies, the FBI and the CIA, and how well they work together in running spies against terrorist organizations in the United States and abroad.

Chapter Eight

Intelligence Failures
and Politicization

L et's start from today's current perception of U.S. intelligence. After the failure to warn of the 9/11 attacks, the WMD fiasco in Iraq, and the five official reports written about one aspect or another of these failures in the aftermath, the intelligence community's current reputation is not healthy. At the outset I should like to dispute several of these negative perceptions, and conclude by asking if political pressure from above caused some of the intelligence community assessments to be so widely off the mark.

The failure to warn of the 9/11 hijackings *was* an intelligence failure, without any question. But it was not just a failure of the intelligence agencies as the commentariat so often assumes. As Harlan Ullman, a scholar at the Center for Strategic and International Studies in Washington, wrote in an op-ed piece for the *Financial Times* in October 2001, 9/11 was more precisely a failure of *intellect* than of the intelligence agencies. None of us "wrapped our heads around" the proposition that a band of civilian hijackers would have the skill and tenacity to train for two years in the United States, some living among us with their families; take practice runs on the eventual suicide flights, carrying box cutters to test the security screening; and finally commandeer four civilian jetliners and use them as WMD on three of America's iconic buildings. It was breathtakingly daring, as well as horrifically effective. As most after-action accounts of the responses to the hijackings have noted (particularly Richard Clarke's *Against All Enemies* and the *9/11 Commission Report*), in addition to the intelligence agencies, nobody else in authority had had an inkling—not the airlines, not the FAA, not the military, not immigration—and it was unclear what they should do in the aftermath. It was a total surprise, even though Tom Clancy had written a novel about such an attack; there had been the foiling of the Bojinka plot to hijack transoceanic airliners in the Philippines in 1995; and the French had recently talked down a hijacked civilian airliner in Marseilles, heading from North Africa, allegedly aiming to crash into the Eiffel Tower in Paris. The after-action reports on 9/11 all pointed to discrete aspects of preparations for the attacks that might have come to the attention of the CIA or the FBI but that were not noted at the time for their intrinsic significance, or were not reported by one to the other for it to adjudge and disseminate. The failure of the CIA to pass on its information on two of the eventual hijackers' attendance at an Al Qaeda conference in Malaysia was particularly disturbing. But nothing that I have read has suggested that there was a thread out there that if pulled might have unraveled the whole scheme. September 11 was a surprise, and, as Judge Richard Posner has remarked in his recent book on the subject, surprises sometimes happen, even when we are anticipating an attack from that quarter.[1] I do not believe the CIA warning to President Bush in August 2001 that Al Qaeda planned an attack in the United States at some point was sufficiently detailed to have constituted a basis for preventive action. I am more concerned by the meeting DCI George Tenet and his top counterterrorist official Cofer Black had with national security advisor Condoleezza Rice some weeks prior, to convey a more specific warning. This appeared to be an intercept about a definite plan to attack the United States.

An example of a comparable intelligence surprise that Judge Posner cites (with which I agree) is that of Pearl Harbor. President Roosevelt knew that Japan was very upset with the United States in 1941 because of our efforts to limit petroleum sales to them in East Asia. By that time, the United States had broken the Japanese diplomatic code but not yet its naval code. There were indications that something was up in terms of imminent war preparations by Japan, but President Roosevelt believed that if there were to be an attack by Japan on the United States, it would start in the Philippines or Singapore. As Roberta Wohlstetter's classic study of the Pearl Harbor attack noted, it was partially a case of American cultural hubris not to believe that the Hawaiian Islands were in play. We were also ignorant of the shallow-draft torpedoes that Japanese air-craft were carrying to attack our naval vessels at anchor.[2]

There are other parallels. The CIA had been warning throughout 2001 that our intelligence friends in the Middle East believed that a major attack on the United States by Al Qaeda was in the offing. Despite the August 2001 briefing provided to President Bush in Texas referred to earlier, the CIA was more focused on the possibility of an overseas attack on an American installation than one in the continental United States, probably because up to this time this is what Al Qaeda had shown itself capable of doing. In the end, however, perhaps we were witnessing a recurrent American blind spot, believing that no halfway sane group of Al Qaeda terrorists would try to bring a suicide attack to our shores. The amateurism of the first World Trade Center assault by Ramzi Yousef in 1993 may have caused our intelligence services to smugly assume that the jihadist terrorists still had a ways to go before they were professional enough to take us on at home, and the oceans separating us from Europe and Asia still counted for something. Even after we became aware of bin Laden's principal lieutenant's involvement in the "Bojinka" plot to hijack commercial airliners in the Philippines and fly them to Washington to crash them on the CIA headquarters and other U.S. government buildings, at around this period, we did not credit the accounts. We thought them too far-fetched and impractical.

One after-action vignette might make the point best, of how unprepared the United States was for suicide hijackings of

American commercial airliners. Tom Pickard, who had been acting director of the FBI after Louis Freeh departed at the end of the Clinton administration, told my Princeton class in the spring of 2006 about the original assumptions the FBI had made as to the manner in which the American and United Airlines pilots had been forced from their seats by the 9/11 hijackers. Bureau agents had initially assumed that the hijackers had used their box cutters or some other weapon to murder the pilots and drag them from behind the controls. A contingent of American and United pilots who were convened by FBI investigators sometime after 9/11 to offer their view of what took place were flabbergasted. No way, they said, could the hijackers have slain the pilots and removed them from behind the controls by force without risking loss of control of the aircraft altogether and crashing them then and there. To a man, according to Pickard, the living pilots believed that their fallen comrades had *voluntarily* relinquished their seats to the hijackers, relying on the then standard belief that hijackers do not want to go down with the planes and can be talked out of their hijacking scheme, or convinced to land at an alternative site, or something of that order. To me this story indicated the degree to which suicide hijacking or bombing was still an alien concept to the entire national defense and civilian airline establishment on September 11, 2001. Although it was a frightening possibility, it was still inchoate and without concrete dimensions to U.S. homeland defenders. We had never before experienced such an attack in the United States.

Often it takes a traumatic event illustrating the way in

which the world has changed dramatically to fix people's attention on what must be done to prepare for and prevent another such occurrence. U.S. intelligence had been tracking Osama bin Laden since he emerged from the campaign to drive out Soviet forces in Afghanistan in the 1980s. We had watched him increase his capabilities, his daring, and his awful accomplishments, from the African embassy bombings in 1998, to the attack on the USS *Cole* in 2000. September 11 was the first look at what nonstate terrorism in the twenty-first-century world could look like on a large scale. Nineteen non-Supermen, reasonably trained and led, could inflict horrific damage on the world's most powerful nation using nontraditional but not nuclear weapons, and at a modest cost of about $500,000. Furthermore, they would not be detected by an intelligence community spending nearly $40 billion a year to prevent such a surprise attack. It has been sobering but, as noted, surprises do happen, and will happen again. The critical point is to make sure you don't suffer a second kick from this particular mule.

Unfortunately, and though largely unrelated to the nature of the 9/11 intelligence failure, along came the Iraqi WMD fiasco in 2003 to finally convince Washington policy makers and the American people of the need to overhaul the entire intelligence structure of the United States. On the surface, the working hypothesis of U.S. intelligence analysts that Iraq possessed substantial unaccounted-for stocks of chemical and biological weapons was unexceptionable. Saddam had considered chemical and biological weapons a major equalizer in his arsenal, to be used against the Iranians and against Shiites

in his own country, and he believed they were the deterrent
that kept the United States from going on to Baghdad after
expelling Iraqi invaders from Kuwait in 1991. Even though
he had been ordered to destroy them by UN resolution in
1991, it was logical that he not let that happen. Our principal
allies and friends in the region believed the same: the UK,
France, Germany, Israel, and Russia, to name a few. The
problem arose from the evidence on which this hypothesis
was grounded. It was all outdated and speculative, and not
based on current eyewitness accounts. As the several after-
action reviewing commissions reported, it was based on
hearsay, worst casing, group think, mirror imaging, and a
lack of imagination–the cardinal deficiencies of the intelligence analysis business. Our last CIA-controlled human
source in Iraq with access to the WMD target departed in
1991 at the time of the first Gulf War, and we were dependent
on cooperating United Nations weapons inspectors after that,
until 1998 when Saddam ordered them out.

A now infamous October 2002 national intelligence estimate (NIE) on Iraqi WMD was commissioned by the Senate
Intelligence Committee expressly to give members of the
U.S. Senate the best intelligence judgment then available on
Saddam's WMD holdings, since the Bush administration
was beginning to argue this issue as the principal casus belli
for an invasion of Iraq. A NIE is normally a premier product
of the intelligence community, formally signed by the director of central intelligence, but this one was drafted in sixty
days, and it showed. It turned the working hypothesis of
Iraq's suspected biological and chemical weapons holdings

into "proven fact," i.e., judgments of the intelligence analytical community, without describing the flimsy and limited evidentiary basis for those judgments. In short, the NIE overstated what it claimed to know and did not indicate what it did not know. The Silberman-Robb presidential commission in 2005 characterized the NIE as a deeply flawed document for these reasons, and made numerous recommendations to improve the integrity and quality of intelligence analysis at the CIA and elsewhere in the community in the course of their report.

There were several other errors in analytical tradecraft that Silberman-Robb also focused on. First was the credibility accorded an important supposed witness to Iraq's mobile weapons laboratories, an alcoholic Iraqi émigré code-named Curveball who peddled a fictitious account of the labs' existence and their configuration for the production of biological and chemical weapons. It turned out that Curveball was a new and unproven German source whose take was supplied to the Defense Intelligence Agency with caveats as to its reliability. Curveball was later found to have been a fabricator.

It now appears that some CIA officials knew that Curveball and his information were no good, and that they attempted to prevent Secretary of State Colin Powell from citing the existence of the mobile labs in his testimony on Iraq's supposed possession of WMD before the United Nations Security Council in February 2003, but to no avail.

Second, and equally damaging because it was also used by Secretary Powell in his UN testimony, was the purchase by Iraq of substantial quantities of aluminum tubes, allegedly for uranium enrichment purposes, according to a majority of the IC. After taking account of the dissenting views of the U.S. Energy Department and the Bureau of Intelligence and Research at State, however, it later turned out that Iraq had likely purchased the tubes as replacement parts for rocket motors.

These were two instances where IC analysis did not serve Secretary Powell and the United States well before the UN. Strong disagreements existed within the intelligence community with regard to both the existence of the mobile labs and the nature of the aluminum tubes. The disputed and erroneous intelligence should not have been included in the most important case the United States was trying to make to the world community about the existence of WMD in Iraq. The fact that they were included raises the question of how and why. Was the IC simply inept or were there other reasons?

How the Iraqi WMD intelligence failures came about has only been examined thus far from the perspective of performance deficiencies in the intelligence agencies themselves. The second phase of the planned Senate Intelligence Committee examination of the Iraqi WMD issue, which was to look at the use to which the intelligence was put by the Bush administration, has not yet been completed. Nor has anybody yet looked systematically at the intelligence with an eye to determining what role the Bush administration may have played in influencing the intelligence judgments. There have been several weighty accusations of improper influence by Vice President Cheney and his staff from knowledgeable CIA insiders, but there has been no formal outside review. This may change with the election of a Democratic-controlled Congress in 2006. New Senate Select Committee on Intelligence Chairman Jay Rockefeller (D–W.Va.) has indicated his intention to go back and examine this issue, but he has been encountering enough difficulty in 2007 just passing an authorization bill for the intelligence community.

Admittedly, the Silberman-Robb presidential commission took a swipe at the issue by asking the relevant intelligence analysts if they believed they were directly pressured by the administration to arrive at a specific conclusion. The analysts demurred, and the commission so noted in their report. The report stated that the commissioners did not find any evidence of Bush administration officials dictating a particular slant or favored outcome to intelligence community studies of the Iraqi WMD issues. But Paul Pillar, the senior IC official on counterterrorism matters during this period, observed in a recent *Foreign Affairs* article that there is much more to politicization of an intelligence study than directing a specific outcome.[3] Pillar noted that in the run-up to the Iraq War there was no doubt as to what the Bush administration wanted and expected respecting U.S. intelligence on the existence of Iraqi WMD and, in his view, it definitely had an impact on how these matters were addressed by the analysts. In short, it did not require Vice President Cheney to be sitting in the room on six occasions with the analysts telling them what to write for the administration to have had a major impact on the outcome.

To me this seems obvious, and is in fact a throwback to the Lyndon Johnson–military view of the importance of North

Vietnamese body counts during the Vietnam War in reflecting America's success. President Johnson strongly favored the higher Defense Department counts of North Vietnamese dead over the more modest CIA numbers as an indication of the United States's successful attrition of North Vietnamese forces, and thus progress toward victory. Enormous pressure was put on CIA analysts in 1968 to "get on board" with the higher DOD numbers—pressure that the CIA for the most part resisted. The argument was quickly knocked into a cocked hat by the communist-led Tet Offensive in early 1968 that showed that whatever the North Vietnamese losses, the communists could still attack at will all over the country.

Political pressure to arrive at an intelligence prediction or judgment that bolsters a president's national security policy is as common in Washington as the springtime arrival of the cherry blossoms, even in a time of war. What is less common is the absence of countervailing pressure from members of Congress who do not agree with the administration view and resent the intelligence books being cooked to produce a phony result. Belatedly, intelligence officers who witnessed instances where IC judgments on Iraq were allegedly influenced by administration pressure are coming forward. If one waits long enough, the truth always seems to come out, even in Washington. My principal concern in this work is to assess what impact the intelligence failures of 9/11 and Iraqi WMD and the possibility of politicization will have on U.S. espionage against terrorist targets in the future. Obviously, if we had had spies in Al Qaeda and Iraq, the chances of such failures would have been diminished.

Or would they? One of the fascinating aspects of Saddam's decision to destroy his biological and chemical weapons stocks after 1991 in order to get out from under UN sanctions is that he apparently never told his generals that this was so. According to the final report of Charles Duelfer's Iraq Survey Group (issued in 2004, with an addendum in 2005), Saddam retained the capability to resume production of WMD but destroyed what he had on the shelf without telling his principal commanders.[4] As the siege of Baghdad approached, the Iraqi WMD cupboard was bare. If Saddam did not entrust this information to his closest confederates, how would any Western spy have acquired the information?

Furthermore, in assessing the totality of the CIA and intelligence community performance in the aftermath of 9/11, there are definite bright spots. The CIA enjoyed considerable success in getting boots on the ground rapidly in Afghanistan because of its long-term relationship with Northern Alliance warlords dating from the successful covert action against the Soviets in the 1980s. The ability of CIA and Special Forces operatives to get the Northern Alliance active against the Taliban early in the fight (with a little help from their briefcases of one-hundred-dollar bills) is now the stuff of legend.

And the IC did stand up to Bush administration efforts to cajole it into support for the erroneous threads of information that suggested there was a Saddam tie to Al Qaeda before 9/11.

Before the administration and Congress, on behalf of the American people, concluded that it was necessary to make wholesale structural changes in the way the intelligence community was configured, they ought to have evaluated its entire performance after 9/11. They should have awaited an examination of what the Bush administration did with the intelligence they were given; how they attempted to prejudge and influence outcomes; and whether, as now appears evident, the decision to invade Iraq had already been made for reasons apart from the existence of Iraqi WMD. The decision to introduce the Intelligence Reform and Terrorism Prevention Act during the 2004 presidential election period was also unfortunate. The perceived need after 9/11 for politicians to not just stand there but *do something* was overwhelming, even if it was too hasty. It is difficult to escape the conclusion that the IC, and particularly the CIA, were unfairly made the sacrificial lambs for much of the perceived inadequacies of the U.S. government in preventing 9/11 and avoiding the Iraq War. This will have destructive consequences for the effort to recast and improve the way the United States goes about collecting and analyzing intelligence on jihadist terrorism in the future.

Chapter Nine

The CIA in Transition

1991 to the Present

W hen I walked back into the original headquarters building in Langley in 1990, after having been confirmed as the first presidentially appointed inspector general of the CIA, I was shocked. I had departed in 1982 to resume a law practice after having served as legislative counsel to DCI admiral Stansfield Turner and subsequently as deputy chief of the Europe division in the directorate of operations.

The CIA had had an inspector general (IG) since the 1950s, but the incumbent had always been a member of the DCI's management team, usually chosen from the cadre of senior managers in the operations, intelligence, or support directorates. As early as the Church Committee investigations into

agency wrongdoing in 1976, however, the Congress had believed that the IG function at the CIA should be strengthened,
because of the difficulties of ensuring accountability in an otherwise unaccountable secret agency. Nothing came of the idea
until the Iran-Contra fiasco in 1988, when the congressional
committee looking into the matter concluded that the CIA IG
might have prevented the abuse if that office had possessed sufficient authority and independence from the director and the
administration to follow the investigative trail where it led. By
that date, presidentially appointed, independent inspectors general had been established by statute in most government departments and agencies in Washington to combat fraud, waste,
and abuse. It was a kind of cottage industry. Over the initial
objections of the DCI and the president, a statutory inspector general was accordingly proposed by the Senate Intelligence Committee and enacted into law in 1990, and I was the
first one. My responsibilities were to investigate allegations of
wrongdoing by agency employees up to and including the director; audit all the accounts, and conduct regular inspections of
agency offices, programs, and stations overseas to recommend
the best practices for accomplishment of the CIA mission.

In the eight-year period while I was away the feel of the
CIA had totally changed. To be sure, the portraits of previous
directors of central intelligence still looked down austerely
from their perches on one of the main corridors of the first
floor, and the wall of honor at the entryway displayed several
new names of fallen CIA officers, but the atmosphere seemed
to me to be profoundly different. The sense that this building
kept the most important secrets of the cold war, and was the

seat of the premier espionage service in the world, had disappeared. It had taken on the cast and color of a conventional old-line bureaucracy, more like the Department of Agriculture than the home of an elite spy service.

Now there was a big CIA souvenir store on the first floor where you could purchase golf balls, with the CIA logo staring at you as you attempted to sink a seven-foot putt. (I often mused that if a casual golfer encountered one of these balls lost in the rough of a local golf course, he would probably assume it was transmitting messages about some secret rendezvous of agents nearby.) There were CIA sweatshirts and baseball caps with the logo advertising the fact that a CIA operative was probably standing right before you.

On summer lunch breaks bands came in to serenade the workforce, with patriotic music over the Fourth of July, and senior officials donned chef's aprons to flip burgers for their junior employees. There was nothing intrinsically wrong with any of these efforts to humanize the place a little, but in time it led to a belief that our mission was much like that of any other government agency, and our employees were no different than any other. And they possessed the same rights and entitlements as most other civil servants.

The folly of this thinking became manifest four years later when, after a devastating nine-year career of giving every secret he could access to the Soviets, Aldrich Ames was arrested outside his home in Arlington, Virginia, and charged with espionage. Ames was a careless spy who openly abused alcohol, failed to get his contact reports and financial accountings in on time, and regularly slept off boozy lunches at his desk in headquarters with nobody seeming to notice, nor stepping up to complain about his behavior. Heretofore, the clandestine service had considered itself a family, and you were your brother's keeper, because an individual officer's improper behavior with secret information could quite dramatically affect the agency's mission.

Sadly, in the course of time, I had further reason to confirm my first impression. The CIA is a place where the most meaningful personnel information never needs to appear on paper. It is instantly the subject of corridor gossip and surmise. And there are no secrets. The CIA may miss the latest detonation of a nuclear blast by India, or mistake the Chinese embassy for a munitions warehouse in downtown Belgrade, but it is alert to the fall of a paper clip in the office of the DCI. As I took up my new duties, the hallway truth was that in the clandestine service, the formula for advancement had become "screw up and move up." Officers talked about poor espionage tradecraft bringing down an entire spy network in a Middle East adversary without a glove being laid on the case officers and managers who were responsible. In this case, an accommodation address in Europe to which reports in secret writing had been sent had been identified and compromised because of overuse, and by the unique and highly stylized handwriting of the box's principal correspondent. The same accusatory pall of inferior operational security hung over espionage operations against the East German intelligence service, the Stasi, and the Cuban intelligence service, where all of our agents against both targets appeared to have been doubled. That is, while they appeared to be U.S. agents, in fact they were reporting to the East Ger man and Cuban intelligence services. Apparently, we had not been sufficiently skeptical about the circumstances that put these agents in our path and had moved to recruit them without asking hard counterintelligence questions.

What had happened? It took me a big part of my eight-year tour as inspector general to even begin to figure it out.

First, the CIA had perhaps become spoiled by its latter-day spy successes against the Soviet Union. At the outset of the cold war, the security wall with which the Soviets surrounded the USSR and Eastern Europe made espionage recruitments behind the Iron Curtain hard to come by. That situation changed for the better after Stalin's death in 1953 and with the ascendancy of Nikita Khrushchev. The Soviets had become dissatisfied with the drudgery of their everyday lives and the lack of consumer goods in their stores, and they were open to a Western approach. By the time the cold war began to wind down under Mikhail Gorbachev in the late 1980s, the CIA and Western intelligence services generally were recruiting more volunteers as spies than they had need for. By the end, from 1989 to 1991, we were turning away KGB colonels like Vasili Mitrokhin, whom we would have welcomed enthusiastically in the past. Mitrokhin later turned himself over to the British, carrying a voluminous archive of KGB documents he defected with. He supplied UK scholar Christopher Andrew with a wealth of information on KGB activities during the cold war that has since become the subject of two detailed and lengthy volumes.[1]

Ironically, the CIA's success in driving the Soviets out of Afghanistan in 1989 (they invaded in 1979) contributed to a sense of accomplishment and partly offset the CIA's fateful involvement in the Iran-Contra scandal. The result was what you might expect. Many clandestine service officers believed correctly that the United States had won the cold war, and that the CIA had been one of the primary contributors to the victory. The question then became, what is next? Many case officers concluded that it might be collecting intelligence on drugs and crime or industrial espionage, and wanted no part of it. They looked at the actuarial tables regarding their projected life span and concluded that there were other opportunities out in the normal world that they wanted to pursue. In addition, the increasingly globalized nature of the world economy meant that there were quasi-intelligence jobs at comfortable salaries for retirees who had traveled the world and could assess international risk.

Case officers thus retired in greater numbers in the early 1990s than predicted, hollowing out an entire cadre of highly experienced spy runners at senior levels in the agency and taking their experience, languages, and tradecraft with them.

This unexpected development was coupled with the desire of the first Bush and the Clinton administrations and the Congress to give the American people a peace dividend at the cold war's end. As a consequence, by the late 1990s there were 25 percent fewer operations officers in the Directorate of Operations at the CIA than at the beginning of the decade.

The second trauma to affect CIA was an unfortunate coincidence. A downsizing and change in the Directorate of Operations took place at a time when there was rapid turnover at the top. From 1990 to 1998, there were five directors of central intelligence. It would be hard to manage any complex organization of the CIA's size and mission with the turbulence that this pace of instability brought about. The changes were not foreordained. They appeared to take place for perfectly ordinary reasons in the cycle and rhythm of regime change in Washington.

Judge William H. Webster was DCI when I returned in 1990 and, having fought the installation of a statutory inspector general in the beginning, he graciously encouraged my appointment in the end. Judge Webster had been brought in from the FBI after the Iran-Contra scandal in 1988 for the principal purpose of restoring integrity to CIA operations, which he accomplished. As the CIA's moment of crisis passed and it was time to get the agency moving offensively again, to take advantage of the collapse of the Soviet Union and act on lessons learned from the Gulf War, President George H. W. Bush named his deputy national security advisor, Robert M. Gates, to the job.

Gates had been a career intelligence analyst who had advanced rapidly in the Directorate of Intelligence and, with several White House stints, had returned to the CIA during the Reagan administration, eventually becoming the deputy director of central intelligence under DCI Bill Casey. Because of Gates's close relationship to the Reagan White House and to Casey, in the wake of Iran-Contra, with a reputation for a tough line against the USSR, Gates had been unable to gain Senate confirmation to succeed Casey upon his death. His second try was a charm, although closely contested. As director,

Robert Gates determined to reorient the CIA to supply fin-
lslied intelligence to the White House and the Congress that
was timely and in answer to policy makers' pressing concerns, not the cocktail table, nice-to-know stuff that he believed he had seen too much of in the White House during
his time there. Gates's drive to revitalize and make more relevant the intelligence product led him to appoint ten or twelve
task forces of intelligence officers and consumers to report
back to him on a tight schedule, suggesting improvements to
the system.

To many agency employees, no sooner had DCI Gates's
task forces completed their assignment than the 1992 election
brought a change in administration, and Gates was gone.

He was succeeded by Washington lawyer and former
deputy secretary of the Navy R. James Woolsey, Jr., who
brought yet another perspective to the job. He had participated in a high-level review of the overhead satellite reconnaissance program (spy satellites) before reentering government,
and he was determined to get through Congress the satellite
architecture that his blue-ribbon committee had favored. Unfortunately, this was neither the policy of the Clinton administration nor of the Democratic-controlled Congress. DCI
Woolsey wasted a great deal of time and capital on this fight.
When he appeared to shy away from the disciplinary recommendations in the IG's report on Aldrich Ames's treachery,
he lost his support in the agency, the White House, and on
Capitol Hill, and his departure was inevitable.

Woolsey was succeeded by Deputy Secretary of Defense
John M. Deutch, whose tour of duty at the CIA was both

unsuccessful and disruptive. His tenure stands in stark support of the truism that one should never take a high-profile government job that you don't want as a stepping-stone to one you do. Having made some unflattering comparisons between the competencies of military and intelligence officers in favor of the former, Dr. Deutch was a dead letter at the CIA almost from the outset. He too had a number of issues he wanted studied and different emphases he wanted to pursue. Most of them seemed directed at putting the national intelligence agencies (and the CIA in particular) more in thrall to the DOD and in support of the military, never a popular theme at the CIA. After Desert Storm in 1991 Deutch had encountered the determination of the military to provide better tactical intelligence support for the troops, such as live satellite feeds to tanks in the field, and he brought that point of view with him when he arrived from the Pentagon.

By the time Dr. Deutch departed in 1996, the CIA was suffering from task force and change fatigue. In addition, the accumulation of setbacks like Iran-Contra and Ames, plus the emphasis of Woolsey and Deutch on technical collection systems and support for the military, were doing nothing to help the Directorate of Operations transition to new targets.

This institutional unraveling came to a halt for a time with the promotion of deputy DCI George J. Tenet to DCI, to succeed John Deutch. Tenet's past experience did not appear to be the ideal roadmap to arrive at the position of DCI but in this instance the indicators were wrong. A people person who had served as a staff director of the Senate Select Committee on Intelligence (1985–88), Tenet had observed the numerous ways in which Deutch's goals and management style had grated on the agency population. He had served on the National Security Council staff (1993–95) during Woolsey's tenure, and had witnessed the disconnect during that period as well. Tenet was determined to slow down the pace of change and get the headquarters building working together again. In the beginning of his tenure, he was enormously popular with the agency workforce in personal terms, for his offhand manner and approachability was manifest when he walked the halls and ate in the employees' cafeteria. More than anything else that he did, however, Tenet's most important contribution in his early days as DCI was to pick up a despondent Directorate of Operations, the center of the CIA's spying activities. A born operator himself, Tenet convinced the people-savvy spy handlers of the DO that he understood and approved of their mission—recruiting spies—and that he would support them.

I have referred above to the sea change in agency operations brought about by the demise of the Soviet Union and the departure to retirement of many seasoned cold war warriors. In addition, the transition to a new set of targets was a prolonged and bumpy one. It was not until the promulgation of the still-classified Presidential Decision Directive 35 in 1994 that the intelligence community was given its new marching orders. This directive was drafted and coordinated by the National Security Council while George Tenet was its intelligence director. It called on the IC to concentrate its intelligence collection on transnational issues such as the proliferation of weapons of mass destruction (WMD), drug trafficking and international criminal enterprise, and, increasingly, states that supported terrorism.

To do this the DO had to reorient itself in a number of ways. As long ago as 1991, led by Webster's deputy director of operations, Dick Stolz, the DO had embarked upon a housecleaning of unneeded and out-of-date operations by devising a directoratewide asset-validation system. For example, spies who had been recruited to supply information on the transshipment of Soviet arms to help Central American revolutionaries in the 1980s were cashiered as no longer needed if their access could not be shifted to a current intelligence priority.

Some of these changes took place under duress. In 1996, there was a messy brouhaha in which a New Jersey congressman accused the agency of maintaining on its payroll a Guatemalan military officer who had participated in the murder of a U.S. innkeeper in Guatemala. The CIA IG and the president's Intelligence Oversight Board (IOB) conducted separate eighteen-month investigations to determine whether the accusation was true. The IG and IOB both found that the report cited by Representative Torricelli (D–N.J.) was erroneous, but the agency was criticized for not keeping its congressional oversight committees fully and currently informed on this operation, as required by law. The bureaucratic outcome was even more unfortunate. Responding to congressional pressure, and to the belief that some DO officers had not been held personally accountable for the Aldrich Ames betrayal (arrested in 1994), in the aftermath of the Guatemala affair DCI Deutch fired several senior operations officers serving in Latin America. This shocked and disgusted the workforce because the DCI was simultaneously engaged in an effort to urge the DO to engage in greater risk taking to collect more intelligence information on so-called hard targets such as terrorists and nuclear weapons proliferators. To make matters worse, Dr. Deutch had promulgated a DCI regulation requiring senior-level headquarters approval for any DO attempt to recruit as a spy an individual possessing a poor human rights or a criminal record. Although the new regulation was doubtless intended as a sanity check following the asset-validation exercise the DO had already engaged in—i.e., if a human rights abuser otherwise had access to priority intelligence, permission to move along and recruit him would be quickly granted—that point was missed at the operational level. Spy runners in the field always have more to do than there is time in which to do it, so rather than pursue a target that would require a high-level debate and lengthy exchange of cable traffic with headquarters, case officers would avoid the issue altogether in the pursuit of other targets.

In the agency and outside, when the Deutch regulation became manifest, it was quickly the subject of ridicule. It was sarcastically noted that important intelligence information seldom was obtained from choirboys.

Into this highly demoralized organization rode new DCI Tenet, who proceeded to enfold the Directorate of Operations in a big affectionate bear hug. He made it a point to tell the agency's spy runners that he understood what they did for a living, and the risks they took, and would stand behind them with the president and Congress, and with the American people. He kept his word, and the new approach worked for a while, until the events of 9/11 and Iraqi WMD overwhelmed even the breadth of George Tenet's heartfelt commitment.

Nevertheless, the agency seemed to be getting back into the basic blocking and tackling of espionage operations at the beginning of his watch. But a third, disquieting, long-term development undercut Director Tenet's efforts prior to September 11. The CIA and its skills and attributes as a tool of U.S. foreign policy were no longer as appealing to presidents as they once had been. Presidents had been markedly turning away from the CIA since the end of the cold war.

When the Soviet Union was America's premier intelligence target prior to its collapse in 1991, the CIA and other IC agencies held a near monopoly on reliable intelligence information about critical aspects of that country's military posture and other significant aspects of Soviet and Soviet bloc power. As a totalitarian state that thawed somewhat toward the end, it was impossible to know what weapons the Soviets were testing and/or deploying unless you stole the information through spying, human or technological. Even on other important matters such as oil and gas production, the Soviets published no reliable statistics so, for example, the estimates of Soviet oil and gas reserves contained in President Carter's National Energy Plan of 1977 were obtained from the CIA.

Much of that changed under Gorbachev, with the result that the centrality of CIA spying to U.S. government understanding of what was taking place in foreign countries critical to America's national security changed with it. Indeed, the IC was severely criticized in 1990 for failing to underscore how weak the civilian economy and infrastructure of the USSR had become in its final days. Around 1994–95, there arose multiple alternative sources of information to that acquired by espionage, such as the Internet and modern media outlets such as Al-Jazeera, in regions that had never been able to afford them before. The result was a virtual explosion of open source material for the policy maker to consume and to understand. To be sure, the CIA and IC were still responsible for tracking other rogue states that had no intention of sharing their national defense secrets with the United States or anyone else—countries such as Libya, Iran, Iraq, North Korea, and even China. But now there was competition in the intelligence information marketplace. As far as fast-breaking events are concerned, the CIA is hard-pressed to outpace CNN or the Internet for headline news, and it should not even try.

Furthermore, a U.S. president leading the most powerful nation in the world is constantly beset by suitors and others who want to convey information to him, in order to gain his attention and support. The intelligence community retained its responsibility for analyzing and organizing the intelligence information that was so much more readily available than before, but the critical importance of its *espionage* role for the formulation of national security policy appeared to have diminished substantially after 1991 and before 9/11.

Consequently, when President George H. W. Bush was contemplating how to remove Manuel Noriega from Panama in 1989, or how to get Saddam Hussein out of Kuwait in 1991, he considered covert action but decided on the military option instead. Likewise, President Clinton had hoped to concentrate on domestic issues as president but agreed to try an "overt" covert action to drive Saddam out of power, in the mid-nineties with the help of the Kurdish-dominated north, that failed miserably. After the bombings of the U.S. embassies in Nairobi, Kenya, and Dar es Salaam, Tanzania, in 1998, President Clinton became obsessed with Osama bin Laden but was never able to rely on IC proof that he was behind all of the terrorist incidents ascribed to him, nor to believe that the CIA had a surefire way to take him out. Finally, despite bin Laden's success in ever bolder terrorist acts against U.S. interests prior to President George W. Bush's election (such as an attack on the USS *Cole* in Yemen in October 2000), the new president found no time to concentrate on the implications of the intelligence about bin Laden's terrorist plans against the United States domestically until after the horrors of 9/11.

Such presidential disinterest toward espionage has institutional consequences. It surely contributed to the decisions of unusual numbers of clandestine service officers to retire after 1991, and doubtless affected the decisions of many prospective candidates not to come in. Several career trainee classes in the DO had dwindled to low double digits before 9/11. A prominent U.S. senator and former member of the Senate Intelligence Committee, Daniel Patrick Moynihan, had even recommended dismantling the clandestine service and returning the agency's analytical functions to the State Department after the Soviet Union's collapse. Senator Moynihan had become so disgusted by the CIA's failure to understand and report on the rottenness of the Soviet economy prior to its disintegration in 1989 that he had lost faith in the IC's ability to do its job.

To be fair, the end of the cold war brought a decline in interest in the federal service generally. Presidential candidates, Democratic and Republican, have been running against the federal government since Jimmy Carter, and the constant negative drumbeat has taken its toll. The "best and brightest" students have not been attracted to federal service as they were during the Kennedy era, when government was considered an honorable calling. The CIA's spy service suffered less than most in this general retreat from government, but it suffered some nonetheless, until 9/11.

The fourth major change that I observed in the CIA, where I had worked in the early eighties and before, was a direct result of the first three. A spy bureaucracy that had grown enormously under DCI Casey became increasingly averse to risk. This aversion to risk has been often remarked upon since, and has been attributed to increased congressional oversight in the wake of hearings by the Church and Pike committees in the mid-1970s (see Chapter 10) and to the presidential executive orders governing intelligence activities that arose from them. More will be said about this in the next chapter, but for now, that reading is not particularly accurate. Certainly, increased accountability to Congress and the executive led to the introduction of more process, and more consultation with the agency's lawyers, before a highly sensitive operation was approved and undertaken in the 1980s and thereafter. In my judgment, this was all to the good if the kibitzing was proactive and designed to make the operation more effective as well as legal.

No, the bureaucratic overlay and risk aversion I caught sight of in the 1990s seemed to occur at least in part because we had forgotten how to play the espionage game. Moscow rules had vanished. Bread-and-butter clandestine tradecraft was overlooked or simply forgotten in the rush to make a spy recruitment that might lead to a promotion. Unheard-of lapses occurred such as case officers using official phones to arrange agent meetings and then meeting in tightly monitored parts of an important European capital where they could be readily observed. Senior spy runners mixed unilateral agent meetings with liaison responsibilities in a major third world country with a sophisticated intelligence service monitoring the whole sorry affair.

Meanwhile, directors of central intelligence during this period were not minding the store. Perhaps the door to the DCI's office was revolving so rapidly that there was no time to settle in, but Jim Woolsey concerned himself with the architecture of spy satellites and John Deutch was concentrating on how to get back to the Department of Defense. During these years I was more than once tempted to echo Casey Stengel's frustration about the early New York Mets: "Can't anybody play this game?" None of these fundamental lapses in spy tradecraft was directly attributable to Senator Church, or to increased executive and congressional oversight. When this noticeable atrophying of basic case officer skills was combined with Deutch's injunction to seek high-level approval of operations to recruit agents with dirty hands, it's a wonder the CIA recruited anybody of significance in the 1990s.

At the same time that tradecraft issues were presenting themselves, the spy service was downsizing, by design as well as unintentionally. The tooth-to-tail ratio (i.e., the ratio of seasoned operations officers to support personnel) diminished substantially in the 1990s. There were not enough capable, experienced case officers to fill important overseas posts. And the work was becoming considerably more difficult, with increasing risk of personal criminal exposure if an operation went awry. Could a case officer even approach a potential agent in a terrorist organization who might sometime in the past have participated in the planning or execution of a plot that resulted in the death of an American citizen? Did such an attempt require prior approval of the Department of Justice's Criminal Division? Could Justice say no on nonoperational grounds? Operating against the terrorist target presented many such questions. The CIA had dodged a bullet in the Torricelli-driven Guatemalan accusation of wrongdoing mentioned earlier, but what if the IG investigation had shown that the American source in Guatemala had in fact participated in the killing of the U.S. citizen? Before 9/11 many in the spy service would have pursued less important targets who did not raise these troublesome issues of reporting to law enforcement and increased personal accountability.

The growing lack of experienced spy runners took its toll

on headquarters' operational support as well during this period. Because of the risk that U.S. official installations overseas might be overrun like the U.S. Embassy in Tehran in 1979 (or bombed like the embassies in Kenya or Tanzania in 1998), it had become the rule that very limited quantities of operational records would be retained abroad, counting on headquarters to preserve the historical record of operations older than six months. To do this effectively, however, the desks at Langley had to be manned by officers who knew where and how to look for the necessary records. They had to have served on the desk long enough to develop a strong familiarity with the overall scope and particulars of sensitive operations in the field so that they might serve as the institutional backup for the field station, and for the chain of command at headquarters if questions arose. (The inspector general found this circumstance sorely lacking in the Guatemala case.)

The sum total of these observations about the condition of the nation's premier spy organization during the period from the fall of the USSR to September 2001 is that it was in major transition. We had not fully grasped the nation's post–cold war espionage needs, and were largely adrift until a year or two prior to 9/11. The clandestine service hollowed out, DCIs came and went, and presidents cared less and less about espionage. The result was predictable. As a generalization, the CIA and the intelligence community were largely unprepared for the enormous change in spy work that jihadist terrorism and post–cold war changes in the world would bring about in the twenty-first century.

The next question is: What structural and programmatic changes needed to be addressed to make espionage effective against this new threat? And have the Intelligence Reform and Terrorism Prevention Act of 2004 and other earlier changes succeeded in bringing this about?

Chapter Ten

Intelligence Reform

It would be a mistake to think of intelligence reform after the cold war as having begun in the wake of the 9/11 intelligence failures. Its roots go back more than thirty years prior, in the congressional and executive branch reaction to the revelation of the family jewels by reporter Seymour M. Hersh in a series of articles in *The New York Times* in December 1974.

Hersh reported that on a number of occasions since its creation in 1947, the CIA had exceeded its mandate and engaged in unauthorized and illegal activities involving U.S. citizens. He pointed to instances of opening mail posted to the USSR from U.S. correspondents; surveillance of American anti–Vietnam War demonstrators in the United States; experiments with mind-expanding drugs such as LSD on unsuspecting agency employees; and assassination plotting against foreign leaders; among other sensational revelations. In early 1975, the Ford administration convened a presidential commission on CIA activities within the United States headed by Vice President Nelson Rockefeller to look into the revelations, and the Congress quickly followed with investigations in each body, the Church Committee in the Senate and the Pike Committee in the House. Hearings went on for the better part of a year, culminating in the issuance of a report by the Church Committee in 1976 that quickly became the basis for reform.[1]

From the vantage point of the present, the major impact of the several inquiries was the establishment of more systematic legislative and executive branch oversight of the intelligence community. The CIA had been knocked off the pedestal of omnipotence and omniscience it had arguably enjoyed since its creation. To many observers within the IC and without, this change was long overdue. Congress had up to this point scarcely looked at the annual CIA budget, and usually limited its inquiries to asking DCIs whether they were getting enough money to accomplish their considerable goals. Senator Leverett Saltonstall, a patrician Republican from Massachusetts sitting on the Defense Subcommittee of Appropriations in charge of the agency's budget, once famously halted a CIA briefer from giving him the name of a certain operation by saying he did not want to know, since he did not want to take the chance of revealing it unintentionally.

However, the Vietnam War had shattered the nation's trust in its government, and the CIA was not immune to this radical change in the way it was received on Capitol Hill. In addition, President Nixon had not helped the agency by dragging it into the plot to remove President Salvador Allende from office in Chile, without telling his own Secretary of State, William P. Rogers, much less anyone in Congress.

In a harbinger of what was to come, Congress approved an amendment to the Foreign Assistance Act of 1961, the Hughes-Ryan Act of 1974. This required the president to *find* that any operation not solely for the purpose of collecting necessary foreign intelligence (a euphemism for covert action) was in the national security interest of the United States, and report such a finding to the relevant committees of the Congress (which at that moment numbered about twelve; so much for plausible denial!) before the operation was commenced. In fact, the agency rank and file were pleased for the most part by the passage of the Hughes-Ryan Act because it squelched subsequent chatter in the Church Committee that the CIA was "a rogue elephant" operating on its own in covert action operations. The amendment made clear what the CIA had insisted upon all along, that the CIA worked for the president, and whatever it did was authorized by the president. The Hughes-Ryan Act further substantiated that point in writing, with the requirement for the first time that all future covert action operations would have to be the subject of a written presidential finding.[2]

The Senate Select Committee on Intelligence was created in 1975 and the House Permanent Select Committee on Intelligence in 1977. The memberships of both committees were to rotate every seven years, and are chosen from the standing committees of the House and Senate that are deemed to have relevant expertise to oversee intelligence operations: Judiciary, Armed Services, Foreign Relations, and Appropriations.

The committees are intended to be bipartisan, the Senate Committee being provided with by a chairman and vice chairman, instead of chairman and ranking minority member. Their establishment created an entirely new oversight process for U.S. intelligence, essentially putting espionage operations into the same annual authorization and appropriations cycle as that affecting every other executive branch department. For the first time the Congress's position as a consumer of intelligence was also established, so the executive would have a much tougher time of keeping it in the dark on sensitive operations. It may still have been true that the CIA's primary constituent remained the president, but it had new and not yet fully defined responsibilities to the Congress as well. The extent of the Congress's role to monitor and approve intelligence activities remains in dispute to the present day in the war on terrorism, as the flap over warrantless domestic surveillance by the NSA has underscored.

No less significant to the evolution of the CIA during the period of investigations in 1975 was its changing position in the executive branch. The Ford administration cleverly sought to cut the ground out from under any potential legislation emerging from the Church and Pike committees' investigations by drafting an executive order of its own, thenceforth governing intelligence activities. In time the Ford executive order became the charter for the CIA that the Congress was incapable of passing. It specified, for example, that the CIA was not authorized to assassinate political leaders either directly or through surrogates. Although the Church Committee subsequently found that the CIA had never been successful in carrying out an assassination plot against a foreign political leader, the Ford executive order made it clear that this was not to be the business of U.S. intelligence anyway. It established other duties and responsibilities for the CIA, but not in a statutory framework that might have been much harder to alter if circumstances changed.

Both Presidents Carter and Reagan retained Ford's executive order's approach to governing intelligence activities, with small refinements of their own but no earth-shaking changes. Meanwhile, as the administration hoped, the steam went out of the National Intelligence Reorganization and Reform Act of 1978 (S. 2525/H.R. 11254) proposed by the Church Committee, when the Soviets invaded Afghanistan in 1979. The Congress and President Carter decided that there might be some use for a reasonably unfettered espionage agency after all.

In 1980, the Congress settled for a new provision in the Intelligence Authorization Act calling on the DCI to keep the congressional oversight committees "fully and currently informed" of all intelligence activities, including covert actions. The language was taken from the Atomic Energy Act of 1954, and has had a storied history on Capitol Hill. It has worked reasonably well, because a special provision was written in permitting the executive some flexibility in the timing of notification of highly sensitive covert action operations. The executive has seventy-two hours to provide notice in the event a president does not wish to give prior notification.[3]

The point is that today the commentariat (*The Weekly Standard* and other neoconservative organs and adherents and their congressional allies) that wants the CIA unleashed quickly turns back to the Church Committee–era reforms to explain the lack of success in espionage operations in recent CIA history, as they see it. If there was no humint prior to 9/11, or not enough flowing from Afghanistan or Iraq, there is a tendency to ascribe it to the alleged disemboweling of the CIA after Church. It is asked, how can a spy agency perform its mission in front of an anxious, micromanaging Congress in a regulatory scheme designed by executive branch lawyers?

I would argue just the contrary. The opposite is what has happened. As counterintuitive as it may sound, by gaining a fully articulated oversight structure in the Congress with presidential findings required for all covert actions, the responsibility for spying that takes place within the boundaries of our constitutional system is more readily assured (or as much as it can be if the players perform their assigned roles). CIA spy runners know that their most challenging missions have been the subject of presidential findings and briefed in secret to the two intelligence committees of the Congress; or if the operation is particularly sensitive, to the "gang of eight."[4]

To be sure, there are more eyes on the spies than formerly, and thus more potential for damaging leaks from Congress, but the track record since 1975 seems to suggest otherwise. Since that time the most damaging leaks have come from the executive branch, from intelligence officers or administration operatives who disagree with the policy behind the spying or covert action, rather than from a more vulnerable Congress. At all events this is how our system is intended to operate. With respect to the issues of account-ability and congressional oversight, President Reagan had the concept right: "trust, but verify." That is especially true in the secret world of espionage.

From the viewpoint of the spy runners involved, it's not even a close question. Case officers know that they are far less likely to be victimized after an unsuccessful operation if the established processes of congressional oversight and exec-utive branch accountability are in place than if they are not. Just ask the unfortunate authors of the so-called Central American assassination manual uncovered in the mid-1980s how far up and down the chain of command the blame for that flap was shared, and you will understand. It was the lonely field operative who paid the price. Or those who took the fall for the agency's role in the Iran-Contra mess. One wonders what is in store for the case officers and interroga-tors in the CIA secret prisons during the war on terror now that the prohibition against cruel and inhumane treatment under Common Article 3 of the Geneva Conventions of 1949 was found to be the law of the land in *Hamdan v. Rums feld*. Increased congressional and executive branch oversight of the spies has made for better and more confident espi-onage rather than the other way round.

In the years after Iran-Contra, the Congress further refined and tightened up the oversight process, passing legislation that forbade the president from attempting covert actions incongru-ent with stated U.S. foreign policy goals. After seeing the exec-utive branch try to move the Iran-Contra effort into the National Security Council to avoid the reporting and other

constraints that affected the CIA, the Congress also passed legislation making the CIA the default instrument for covert ac
tions, unless the president decides otherwise and notifies the
Congress. Realizing that highly sensitive foreign intelligence-
gathering operations could entail as much risk to U.S. foreign
policy equities and assets as a covert action operation, the Congress insisted that it be briefed on these prior to inception as
well. I believe the NSA effort at tracking communications from
known Al Qaeda communications nodes into the United States
without obtaining Foreign Intelligence Surveillance Court
(FISC) warrants should have been briefed to the full intelligence committees pursuant to this law. It is a well-established
practice that would doubtless have excited less opposition than
the mismanaged failure to consult them all for three years.

Once again, those of the view that the spy agencies have
been unwisely constrained by these new strictures have had a
field day complaining about them. But most spy professionals
recognize that these requirements may protect them from becoming pawns in an after-action blowup, if the executive is
tempted to move too quickly to use its clandestine arm to
"fix" something that it would never ask the military or the
State Department to do overtly. Not only is prior notification
required, in my judgment, for hostile interrogations in secret
prisons, but it is also necessary in cases of "extraordinary rendition" such as those that were played out in Italy, Germany,
and Canada in 2006 and 2007. The United States has been
greatly embarrassed by its reported decisions to abduct an
Egyptian cleric from the streets of Milan; by sending Canadian citizen Maher Arar to Syria to be tortured; and most re-

cently for kidnapping a German citizen in Macedonia and sending him to Afghanistan for interrogation. Perhaps if the oversight committees had been informed they might have counseled against or even sought to prohibit a practice that our allies and neighbors in the world are increasingly objecting to.

For that is the real issue at play. As a constitutional democracy, the United States should not wish to be using its department of dirty tricks mindlessly, to carry out ill-considered missions that shock the conscience and are authorized simply because there is believed to be no audit trail and no outside review.

It's a fine line. I oppose vehemently the so-called overt covert action, in which the executive branch uses the statutory mechanisms of secret presidential findings, with notice and debate limited to the intelligence committees (that takes place for purposes of notification, not approval), in order to embark upon a covert action that it then proceeds to talk about as if it had been fully debated in the executive branch and throughout the halls of Congress. This was the process used almost by happenstance in the 1980s, in the case of U.S. support for the Contra rebels in Nicaragua by the Reagan administration, in which both the president and his national security advisor commented on U.S. support for the brave Nicaraguan "freedom fighters." No such pretense of secrecy was even attempted during the Clinton administration when assistance was provided "covertly" to anti-Saddam elements in exile in Europe and in the Kurdish north of Iraq, yet was debated openly in the House and Senate when it appeared not to be effective. My view is that the procedures developed to bottall the debate clause in the Congress with respect to covert action spy operations should be reserved to those we intend to keep secret, not to those to which we are giving a halfway kind of cover because they might prove politically controversial or internationally embarrassing if they were revealed. To severely curtail the scrutiny normally given to foreign policy actions on the assumption that the hand of the United States is intended not to show and then turn around and debate the policy openly is unwise and counterproductive.

In sum, the pre-9/11 intelligence "reforms" that grew out of cold war excesses, or refinements to the covert action process based on experience since 1974, have presented no impediment to CIA case officers engaged in traditional espionage. The congressional oversight process, and the system of executive branch accountability through inspector general and general counsel review of prospective sensitive operations, has been for the most part a healthy check on a tendency to use covert action operations to solve problems that can't be attacked overtly, and may not be reachable covertly either. As noted previously, in an age of the twenty-four-hour news cycle and the proliferation of news outlets worldwide, the challenge of mounting a covert action the size of the CIA's support for the anti-Soviet mujahideen in future seems daunting.

My attitude toward the reforms sought for espionage after 9/11 and the Iraqi WMD fiasco are not nearly so benign. As stated earlier, I am in the Posner camp. The changes mounted to the intelligence community by the Intelligence Reform and Terrorism Prevention Act of 2004 seek to remedy personnel and programmatic deficiencies with structural fixes. In most cases I find them ill conceived and likely to enhance the bureaucracy rather than produce better intelligence. I daresay the first director of national intelligence (DNI), John Negroponte, concluded the same thing; hence his departure to the second-ranking position in the Department of State after little more than twenty-two months as DNI.

The three most important after-action reviews of 9/11 and Iraqi WMD made some excellent suggestions for improvements, many of which could have been implemented by the president without seeking legislative change.

The ad hoc congressional review that reported out first, in December 2002, pointed to the three or four instances prior to 9/11 where information sharing between the CIA and the FBI did not take place as it should have, and underscored the point that in the war on terrorism it is critical that cooperation be seamless between these two most important agencies in the international and domestic espionage and counterespionage fields. September 11 showed that the distinction between foreign and domestic intelligence gathering has disappeared. What began as talk in a Hamburg mosque quickly became a terrorist plan of attack in New York City and Washington, D.C., so information sharing was imperative. The Intelligence Reform and Terrorism Prevention Act of 2004's effort to legislate this by creating an "Information Sharing Environment" in the IC is ludicrous and sophomoric.

President Bush acted on this issue quickly and appropriately after 9/11 by holding regular meetings with his DCI and FBI director, and used the chain of command to ask them if they were talking to one another on the terrorist concerns of the day. Civil servants usually respond rapidly to an expression of presidential concern.

The 9/11 Commission reported next, in the summer of 2004, in an elegantly drafted volume readily available to all Americans. The report did not offer much new evidence about the circumstances surrounding 9/11 that had not already been mentioned in the ad hoc congressional report, but it had greater visibility because of the push given to it by the 9/11 families, who had lost loved ones in the attacks (not to mention the televised committee hearings and the media appearances of chairmen Thomas H. Kean and Lee H. Hamilton). It made the crucial pitch for a director of national intelligence who would be, in the metaphor of the report, the attending physician who would supervise the work of the specialists (the fifteen separate intelligence agencies in the IC) and pull it all together so that it would make sense and meet the country's needs. But we already had a national intelligence director in the person of the DCI. The problem had been that since the CIA had been created in 1947, few DCIs had chosen to exercise extensively their DNI responsibilities, because they were simultaneously discharging the role of CEO of the Central Intelligence Agency. To change this no longer acceptable allocation of responsibilities, all the president had to do was tell his DCI that he expected him henceforth to be head of the intelligence community in fact, and leave the running of CIA to his deputy. After all, this was what was done in the bureau with the responsibilities of the director of the FBI. His antiterrorist duties were enhanced, but the FBI still retains its principal criminal investigative mission.

Perhaps the 9/11 Commission decided that there was too much water under the bridge for the DCI to now try to discharge his responsibility as head of the IC. However, the DNI's office as created in the Intelligence Reform and Terrorism Prevention Act seems thus far not to have met the commission's desire to establish one overall leader for the intelligence community. On the one hand, with the necessity of his being the president's chief daily intelligence briefer and adviser, the DNI needs an analytical staff to support him (to be drawn mostly from the CIA). Secondly, he needs to be on-call to answer for the IC before Congress, and to brief it on current intelligence as the senior intelligence official in the executive branch. Third, in order to speak for and guide the work of the IC, he has to figure out how far his authorities extend vis-à-vis the Secretary of Defense for the so-called defense intelligence agencies—DIA, NSA, NRO, and the National Geospatial Intelligence Agency (formerly NIMA, or imagery analysis)—that spend 80 percent of the annual IC appropriation, but whose activities are authorized in the Defense Department budget. Fourth, and only then, will he have time to work on the IC budget and look to the future for coming intelligence needs and challenges. To accomplish these tasks, media reports have it that Ambassador Negroponte had decided he needed a considerable staff of fifteen hundred officers and a more than billion-dollar budget. If true, this looks to many like the creation of a new layer of bureaucracy. It looks like the re-creation of the old intelligence community staff function but with more bells and whistles. It flies in the face of most current business organization theory that reducing layers of bureaucracy is the key to more effective management. Perhaps the DNI could earn his stripes with the rest of the IC if he concentrated on long-range planning and the future needs of the intelligence agencies, but if he becomes just another greedy consumer and critic, and if he cherry-picks IC resources to fulfill his responsibilities to the Congress and the president, there would appear to be very little real value added by his office.

The verdict is still out on the DNI, as a consequence of the Intelligence Reform bill, but it is crystal clear in the case of the CIA. The agency has become the big loser in the legislative effort at intelligence reform. It is a shadow of its former self, with espionage its only national assignment. It is no longer in charge of preparing the President's Daily Brief. The CIA *is* the national *humint* authority, so called, but it is operating outside the sphere of cooperation with the analytical arm of the IC that it took fifty-five years to build up. The spies have become disconnected from the analytical mechanism that coached them on what needed to be collected, what it meant and what it didn't, because it no longer cohabits the Langley headquarters with the analysts who are now advising the DNI.

Finally, the Silberman-Robb presidential commission was the last to report in March 2005. After declaring, as had the

Senate Select Committee on Intelligence and the David Kay commission before it, that the CIA had gotten the Iraqi WMD issue all wrong, it went on to comment on some of the causes of the analytical breakdown and made some solid recommendations for improvements, very few of which the commission believed needed new legislation to bring about. It complained, as the earlier reports had, about groupthink and lack of imagination. It pointed out the tendency of intelligence analysts to view threats in a worst-case manner when confronted with slim evidence, and to substitute or mirror *our* likely responses to a given situation for those in Iraq. A good example was the assumption that Saddam would never liquidate the biological or chemical weapons he had relied on to hold back his toughest foes in years past. On that issue, it did not take into account the pressure Saddam was feeling from Iraqi citizens, especially Shias, because of the deprivations caused by the UN economic sanctions that he believed he had to bring to an end.

Finally, the report stressed that in every case built so extensively on speculation and guesstimate, somebody should be deputized to be the devil's advocate to test out the more unusual hypotheses. The Silberman-Robb commission called for the institutionalization of the A Team/ B Team process of analysis for problems like the one about the existence of WMD in Iraq where the evidence was so old and thin.

Perhaps the Silberman-Robb commission's greatest contribution to this flawed analytical effort was to urge the intelligence analysts to have the courage to indicate when they did not have sufficient evidence to make a judgment and, failing that, to never overstate the evidence behind a given judgment. Again, these are matters of analytical tradecraft and process, not structure.

Not sufficiently emphasized in any of the three critical reports is the matter of understanding the constantly changing and expanding nature of Islamist fundamentalism that underlay the 9/11 attacks. Further, this is not just an espionage issue. For the United States government to be as clueless as it was regarding the frustration and hatred of Osama bin Laden, Mohamed Atta, and his band toward the West, and the United States in particular, and for the United States to believe that in overthrowing Saddam we would be greeted as liberators in Iraq, shows such a fundamental misunderstanding of the radical religious dynamic at work in the Middle East that one wonders where to begin to correct it. The CIA may have known the correct answers but it did not succeed through Tenet or others in penetrating the wall of willful ignorance erected by the administration. All reports and the president have noted the great importance of improving our knowledge of the languages of the region: Arabic, Farsi, Dari, Pashto, etc. No less important is a crash course in cultural understanding. Yet these are not primarily intelligence or espionage issues. They are national challenges to U.S. understanding of the time we are living in and the role of fundamentalist Islam.

It may well be that on many of the key points in the run-up to the Iraq war, the CIA and the IC got it right, as Michael Scheuer, Paul Pillar, and former acting director John McLaughlin suggest in their retrospectives. The CIA certainly never relented on the issue of supposed ties between Saddam and Al Qaeda concerning the planning prior to 9/11. There weren't any. Doubtless, a future examination of the pressure put on CIA analysts to toe the administration line in its intelligence reporting on Saddam will reveal additional instances in which IC reporting was taken out of context or reworked to suit political ends. As noted earlier, that has happened before. What is less acceptable is that CIA and IC sources on both Al Qaeda and Saddam's Iraq were so scanty. As to that, the Intelligence Reform and Terrorism Prevention Act is largely silent in its postmortem and its recommendations for the future.

It remains to explore in the next part the role current U.S. spying capabilities can be expected to play in the early twenty-first century. Can we do better? Is espionage needed in the way it was in the cold war to fight America's current enemies and keep the president and his top policy makers fully informed on national security concerns and developments?

Part Three

---

*Spying in the
Twenty-first Century*

What do the president and his top policy makers need to know in the twenty-first century that can best be acquired by spying? This work so far has concentrated on jihadist terrorism because since 9/11 the United States has been engaged in a so-called global war on terror that has been the United States's top priority. It may well turn out that the war on terror is more akin to the cold war, which lasted for forty-five years, from 1946 to 1991, than anything else.

In any event, it is grandiose and presumptuous for the United States to call the campaigns in Afghanistan and Iraq part of a Global War on Terror because we and the UK are the principal, and increasingly the only, protagonists of this war. Even in the United States, there has been little national commitment to the task beyond the extraordinary sacrifice of the 150,000 soldiers involved in fighting it. There has been little call for sacrifice and none for belt-tightening.

Beyond this war on terror are there other issues, or intentions toward us of other groups, that we can most effectively learn about through espionage? This is a hard question. If effectively carried out, spying on other countries that rival us in their need for primary resources or that aspire to challenge us technologically might be quite useful. Traditionally, the United States has never engaged in industrial espionage as such, as it is impossible to decide to whom in the United States to give the fruits of such an endeavor, if not everyone involved in the particular business enterprise spied upon, and thus impossible to keep it a secret. Nowadays, that problem is further compounded by economic globalization, in which ownership of the most important industrial or scientific enterprises is spread widely throughout the world.

Furthermore, espionage is an expensive, inefficient, and illegal way of gathering national security information. It can only be justified if it is necessary for purposes of national security or defense. Accordingly, jihadist terrorism is a subject which all policy makers and congressional overseers can agree needs to be pursued with every weapon in the U.S. arsenal, including espionage.

That said, the critics have been unanimous after 9/11 and the known mistakes on Iraq that the United States needs more and better humint on Islamist terrorism, especially in the Middle East. My response is simply, of course we do, but before determining what is needed to be successful in meeting current intelligence challenges, we need to face some hard facts: It will be difficult work; it will take time; and it will be piecemeal and unpredictable. Doubtless, it will be invaluable if we can get it, but it is unlikely to come to us in wholesale amounts. Human spying is not a mass-production business. Intelligence information acquired by spies is a product of human nature and behavior. It is not akin to the electronic download from a satellite or the take from an intercepted cell phone conversation. It is most often the result of a bargain or compromise, like those described earlier involving the seven principal motivations for espionage.

As a consequence, the process by which the United States hopes to improve its humint take from terrorists will involve far greater language competency, a deeper understanding of Muslim cultures and the appeal of radical Islamism, and *access*. More important, however, it will require that we project a different image in the Middle East. Currently, because of our presence in Iraq, our support for Israel, and our position as the biggest promoter and beneficiary of economic globalization, we are too often seen as insensitive and even hostile to Islamic culture and interests. We are viewed as hegemonic, imperialist, interested primarily in oil and bases for our armed forces, and in spreading an alien secular culture offensive to traditional Islam. We are not yet perceived as the force to bring hope, peace, and progress to the region. As a consequence, we shall have difficulty filling the role we did during the cold war, as the only acceptable alternative to Soviet expansionism. This time we are the bad guys.

Given the very narrow and unfavorable base from which we start, it will take some time before we shake off the burden of our current reputation unless shortcuts become available. The 9/11 Commission reported that there were only six students

majoring in Arabic studies in American colleges and universities in 2002. This has increased dramatically since the fateful
date of the attacks, but the base is still small. It will still be an
inadequate pool from which U.S intelligence can draw for
many years, even if the president's plan to immediately increase the number of hard-language speakers by 50 percent
goes through. (The recently approved Intelligence Authorization Bill for FY 2008 shows that we are off to a slow start in
building a sharp increase in the number of hard language
speakers.)

Furthermore, there have only been a handful of American
Arabic speakers of any stripe in Iraq since 2003 who could
engage in a colloquial exchange of views on Al-Jazeera. The
Iraq Study Group in its report to the president on December 6,
2006, noted that there were only six fluent Arabic speakers of
the needed proficiency in the Green Zone in Iraq at the time
of their visits.

It makes it very difficult to get close to potential sources of
information in the Middle East if our spy runners don't speak
the languages of the region competently. Gone are the days of
the agency's early espionage operations in the Middle East
when a seasoned intelligence officer could declare that the
only language he needed to gain access was that of money.

There are some potential shortcuts around the current ob-
stacles of language and cultural understanding to better access. The most prominent, of course, and the most secure
would be to recruit more native linguists from the Arab
American community in the United States. This appears to
be taking place but not yet in enormous numbers, because of

security clearance problems, and to some degree disenchantment among some Arab Americans with the U.S. government's policy and strategy in the region. Admiral Mike McConnell, the new director of national intelligence, has pledged to seek to hire more first- and second-generation Muslim Americans. The second shortcut would be greater reliance on friendly intelligence liaison services in the region. More on that later.

Access to potential sources of intelligence information is perhaps harder in the Middle East than elsewhere because of the language, and of religious and cultural differences, but these are not insurmountable. They will be overcome with education and time. More than language and cultural differences, however, there appears to be a considerable disconnect based on perceived unconditional U.S. support for Israel in the region. America's support for conservative regimes in Egypt, Saudi Arabia, and Jordan also does not help in some Islamist quarters. But other regions equally dismissive of American cultural and economic hegemony have found ways to accept the good and dismiss the objectionable from their points of view. In the Arab street this has always been a hard sell for the United States. Fundamentally, it takes a willingness to spend a great deal of time getting to know, empathize, and work with members of a civilization that feels left behind and exploited for its oil without consideration for its religious scruple, ethnic divisions, or cultural heritage. There appears to be little alternative. U.S. spy runners will have to spend the effort and time to get to know, understand, and gain the confidence of Arabs. That is why the simplest and most effective solution is to employ more Arab American case officers in the region.

If that is an accurate reflection of the challenge our spymasters face currently, it is my view that we are unlikely to see a major improvement in the number of Islamist spies recruited just using the techniques elaborated in the seven motivations for espionage described earlier. Ideology, money, intimidation, revenge, excitement, ethnic solidarity, and friendship still count and remain important leverage points for effecting spy recruitments, but they won't be sufficient in an age of holy terror. Classic espionage will have to be leavened by techniques from other disciplines such as law enforcement and the military. As an aftermath to 9/11 and the war in Iraq, successful espionage will result from a combination of skills and attributes, many flowing from new technology and a new sense of teamwork. Let's turn to that now.

Chapter Eleven

Actionable Intelligence and the Role of Law Enforcement, the Military, and Technology

For most of its history America's spies have produced intelligence information on political, military, scientific, and economic subjects considered important to the president's national security responsibilities. In wartime, the focus sometimes narrowed to force protection and other discretely military issues. But national intelligence (as contrasted with departmental intelligence) normally focused on current issues and future developments that the intelligence community believed the president and his senior advisers needed to be apprised of if they were to manage successfully the national security interests of the

United States. In other words, except in times of emergency, the national intelligence product in the past was not primarily action-oriented in a tactical way. It was not particularly geared to order of battle or the force-protection requirements of the military or the tactical and forensic demands of law enforcement. Essentially, it reported on the capabilities of America's rivals or enemies and, where it had the assets, on their intentions.

Intelligence collection now has a much sharper, action-oriented focus. Since the 9/11 attacks the president expects the IC, and the FBI and the CIA in particular, to gather intelligence that will *preempt* or *prevent* future 9/11 attacks. This is more than the CIA's earliest and most significant responsibility to give strategic warning of future Pearl Harbors. It now extends to the timing, nature, and what must be done to stop the attack. The president's expectation is that the IC, using all of its collection antennae, will have as its highest priority the protection of the American people from any significant future terrorist assault.

The IC has a name for this new priority requirement: *actionable intelligence.* And the entity most responsible for gathering, analyzing, and disseminating actionable intelligence on terrorist matters is the National Counter Terrorist Center (NCTC), established by the Intelligence Reform and Terrorism Prevention Act of 2004 and newly located near Tyson's Corner, Virginia.

This center is multijurisdictional as well as multidisciplinary. Its personnel is and will be drawn in future from across the IC. It is a follow-on to the DCI's Counter-Terrorist Center (CTC) set up in 1986 by Bill Casey during the Reagan administration to deal with an earlier era of state-sponsored terrorism. Led by Dewey Clarridge, at the outset the Counter-Terrorist Center was the first IC center that gathered experienced intelligence officers, collectors, and analysts from all agencies involved in tracking potential terrorists, including law enforcement: CIA, FBI, Customs, Immigration, Justice, State, DOD, Coast Guard, and others.

The significance of this historical antecedent is that it was multidisciplinary. Spy runners were taught the rudiments of the rules of evidence, so that captured documents could be preserved in such a way that they could be introduced in court if there were to be a judicial proceeding, as in the trial of Ramzi Yousef in New York in 1996. Law enforcement was reminded that what was possible in procedural terms in the United States might be offensive or would not work in some foreign locales. Most important was the experience of working together shoulder to shoulder, confronting common problems and devising solutions or work-arounds to thwart the terrorist threat. The major difference between the DCI Counter-Terrorist Center and the NCTC is that the DCI is no longer in charge. Civilian intelligence as personified by the CIA is no longer top dog. The leadership and staffing is to be collaborative and collegial, directed by the director of national intelligence and not dominated by one discrete intelligence agency such as the CIA.[1]

In my judgment it will be the NCTC that serves as the model for the sharing of information between law enforcement, intelligence, and the military that Congress and the American people want to see, not a hortatory injunction in the Intelligence Reform and Terrorism Prevention Act to create an "information sharing environment." Professionals share information when it is in their professional interest to do so and they believe they are part of a team.

The DCI Counter-Terrorist Center cut its teeth on some interesting cases in the late 1980s and early 1990s. The Congress had passed a statute after the *Achille Lauro* hijacking in 1985 that made it a federal crime, cognizable in U.S. courts, for a terrorist to kill a U.S. citizen in the course of a terrorist attack anywhere in the world. And our courts would not question how an accused was "rendered" before the bar of U.S. justice. It would try him on the facts of the case.

Therefore, in a number of instances, with the cooperation of friendly foreign governments and intelligence liaison services, the FBI and CIA working as a team were able to snatch suspected terrorists in foreign jurisdictions and render them to appear before federal courts in the United States. Ramzi Yousef and Mir Amal Kansi, the CIA headquarters shooter, were both brought back to the United States from Pakistan in this way, the latter to face trial in state court in Fairfax County, Virginia. Similar renditions took place after the U.S. embassy bombings in Kenya and Tanzania in 1998. Judicial renditions are examples of actionable intelligence at work in its most acute form.

The USA Patriot Act, passed little more than a month after 9/11, added further support to the possibility of collecting more actionable intelligence. Central to the changes brought about by the Patriot Act were revisions to the Foreign Intelligence Surveillance Act of 1978 (FISA). FISA had created a special court that could issue warrants in secret to the U.S. government to conduct electronic surveillance of spies suspected of operating in this country. The basis for granting the warrants in these cases was thought to be less onerous than the "probable cause" standard appropriate for ordinary criminal prosecutions in U.S. courts that were governed by the Fourth Amendment prohibition against "unreasonable searches and seizures" in the U.S. Constitution. Further, no notice need be given to those under surveillance afterward, if there was no criminal prosecution. The theory behind permitting a looser standard was that the surveillance information was being collected for intelligence-gathering purposes *not* criminal prosecution.

The Patriot Act amended FISA to extend the warrants to those suspected of planning to commit terrorist acts in the United States. It retained the looser standard but recognized that there was no prohibition against using the information collected in a criminal prosecution. In order to prevent FISA from becoming a way around the Fourth Amendment requirement of probable cause, the Patriot Act specified that prevention of terrorism had to be "a significant purpose" for seeking the warrant from the FISA court.

This procedure is still not without its critics, but the Bush administration has leapt beyond this issue since 9/11 by using electronic surveillance through NSA computers in the United States to monitor phone calls coming from suspected Al Qaeda sources outside the United States to recipients inside. No warrants for this surveillance were sought from the FISA or any other court, probably because at the time of collection the United States government did not know who the U.S. contacts might be. It looks as if the solution to this problem may be the interposition of the FISA court into the process of overseeing the warrantless surveillance to make certain U.S.

civil liberties are not unreasonably abridged. If so, it is too bad this procedure was not suggested to or worked out with the Congress in the first place.

In addition to amending FISA, the Patriot Act strengthened authorities available to the U.S. government to trace and prevent terrorist financing worldwide. This appears to have had some recent success in the blackballing of certain banks that financed illegal transactions for North Korea and Iran. Further, the act authorized pen-registers and trap-and-trace devices to capture parts of telephone and Internet communications; it also changed the law on telephone and wireless surveillance to cover the individual using the communications device rather than the device itself. As with many of the changes brought about by the Patriot Act, they had long been sought by law enforcement and the IC, but it took the trauma of 9/11 to supply the pressure to get them enacted.

A key push to greater information sharing between the FBI and the intelligence community and other agencies concerned with terrorism was the Patriot Act's alteration of rule 6(e) of the Federal Rules of Criminal Procedure (FRCP). The amendment permitted the FBI to share grand jury information from terrorist prosecutions with the IC and other agencies interested in the case. Former DCI Jim Woolsey had lamented the CIA's inability to gain access to Ramzi Yousef's grand jury testimony in 1995, which he believed contained lead information to other terrorists. The change to the FRCP took care of that problem.

Although 9/11 showed that the divide between foreign and domestic intelligence collection responsibilities was no longer valid or realistic, not all the legislation keeping the jurisdictions between the CIA and the FBI separate was changed to reflect that new reality. Because in creating the CIA, President Truman had not wanted to create a U.S. "Gestapo" in 1947, the National Security Act of that year establishing the CIA contained a provision preventing the agency from being granted any domestic law enforcement or subpoena powers. The upshot has been that there are still limits on what the agency can do to assist law enforcement in the apprehension of terrorists and rendition of them to U.S. courts. That's why the operations to return Yousef and Kansi to the United States from Pakistan were joint efforts of the FBI and the CIA, with FBI agents actually making the arrests. Agency lawyers have always drawn the line on the investigative side at the point at which U.S. attorneys sought to task spy runners to gather evidence abroad against terrorist suspects who are U.S. citizens.

Ironically, with all the other structural changes to the IC sought in the Intelligence Reform and Terrorism Prevention Act of 2004, there was no apparent effort to change this domestic law enforcement prohibition respecting the CIA. My view is that this was probably not an oversight but reflected a continuing concern about the appropriateness of involving agencies stealing secrets overseas in the business of domestic law enforcement, despite the extent to which IC information informed the efforts of the CTC and now the NCTC.

Nonetheless, tactical or actionable intelligence is a major focus of U.S. spying efforts against the terrorist target today, and as noted it will involve teamwork. The contributions of law enforcement and the military in identifying, surveilling, pursuing, and killing or capturing terrorists are now a necessary and accepted part of the intelligence effort.

We have discussed the role of the FBI in overseas renditions, and in working with the CIA to pursue Al Qaeda terrorists operating domestically, based on intelligence warnings gathered overseas. What is relatively recent is the expansion of legal attaché offices in U.S. embassies abroad that perform intelligence functions in addition to representing the Department of Justice in its overseas needs to exchange legal documents, take witness statements, etc. FBI agents abroad give foreign intelligence liaison services a direct tie to law enforcement representatives in the United States, such as the New York City Police Department.

In addition, there was full consideration given at the time of passage of the Intelligence Reform and Terrorism Prevention Act as to whether the United States should remove the FBI altogether from the intelligence game. The 9/11 Commission had looked at creating an American MI-5, a separate domestic intelligence service, paralleling the role of its famous British counterpart. Upon strong representation from FBI director Robert Mueller and the Bush administration, both the commission and Congress relented and backed continuance of the FBI in its domestic intelligence role. But it insisted that the bureau make intelligence a career service and responsibility, along with the traditional crime-busting street agent profile. Counterterrorism would have to become the priority mission for the FBI, surpassing some traditional crime-fighting responsibilities. Further, it would have to create and utilize an intelligence analysis function that would be focused on more than criminal prosecution.

It remains to be seen whether the FBI culture can and will absorb this enormous change, and whether demand will persist for this kind of competency. If it does, what will help immeasurably over time is the FBI seconding its promising agents on rotational duty to the NCTC, as was attempted earlier with the DCI's CTC, and also to the intelligence directorate at the CIA, to bone up on the tradecraft of intelligence analysis.

By the same token, it is imperative to have the CIA send its best and brightest on rotational assignments to the FBI. It will not hurt to have spy runners pursue a crash course on what constitutes legal evidence, and how to manage a hostile interrogation.

For example, if the FBI approach to interrogating prisoners had been followed at Abu Ghraib and Guantánamo, arguably both the military and the CIA might have obtained more intelligence information and drawn less international criticism. The bureau does not believe in the efficacy of coercive interrogations, but prefers to gain the subject's confidence and induce him to confide in the interrogator as one who may have spared him from a more hostile approach, and a longer jail sentence.

Referring to the FBI, DCI John Deutch once laconically noted that "cops are cops," and by implication *not* intelligence officers. This may have been true in a time of classical espionage during the cold war, but the rise of Islamist terrorism and the potential threat it represents to American cities requires a response that combines both the longer range knowledge of the modalities and working assumptions of Al Qaeda with the criminal investigative smarts and forensics of a sophisticated law enforcement organization. Critical to the apprehension of Ramzi Yousef for the first World Trade Center bombing in 1993 was the FBI's ability to find and trace the vehicle identification number on the rented U-Haul van used to transport the explosives from New Jersey to the underground garage of the trade center. Admittedly, it was the amateurism of the bombers, who brought one vehicle back to the rental agency to claim the deposit, that thus led to their arrests, but this could well have gone for naught if the FBI had not uncovered the VIN. Likewise the British police were quickly able to identify the perpetrators of the 7/7 underground bombing in London in 2005 from the video cameras set at the entranceways to the underground stops they used.

Dealing with jihadis adds a military dimension to the intelligence role as well. Two interesting recent books cover the mission of CIA special operations officers in spearheading the U.S. response to the 9/11 attacks in Afghanistan.[2] As one of the titles declares, CIA paramilitary case officers were the "first in" on the ground in Afghanistan after 9/11, more than three weeks ahead of the first uniformed military special forces teams, and their responsibilities were huge. They had to make contact with Northern Alliance representatives who had just lost their longtime commander and hero Ahmad Shah Masood. They had to convince these suspicious Uzbeks and Tajiks that the United States was serious this time about helping them over the long term against the Taliban, and did not intend to bug out as we did in 1992, after the Soviets had departed.

Led by Gary Schroen and then Gary Berntsen, the CIA paramilitary case officers were able to resuscitate the earlier CIA relationship with the Northern Alliance, and using bags full of one-hundred-dollar bills, help equip the mujahedin to fight against the Taliban. It was a skillful employment of three of the principal motivations for espionage—friendship, money, and ideology—to drive this relationship, and it led to the fall of Kabul and the eventual interim NA and U.S. success over Taliban forces in the south around Kandahar.

Interestingly, this formula for success offers promise for the future. Most of Schroen's and Berntsen's teams were ex-military—Army Rangers, Delta Force and Special Forces, and Navy SEALS—who had been through the CIA operations course at the Farm, the agency's training base near Williamsburg, Virginia. Many had been forced by age into desk jobs against their will, or confronted an absence of field billets to continue the paramilitary work they had liked in the military, so they had switched to the CIA. After several tours of duty as paramilitary spy runners, they were able to combine both skills. They were adept at the military arts, but supplemented these talents with hard languages and good report writing abilities.

If the United States finds itself embroiled in future Afghanistans, this model will be hard to beat, especially since it can be deployed so quickly. I believe it was the speed and agility of this CIA paramilitary deployment, code-named Jawbreaker, to Afghanistan that led the Pentagon and the

White House to stand down from following the 9/11 Commission recommendation that all paramilitary intelligence activities be henceforth concentrated in the DOD. By tradition and experience, the CIA deploys faster.

It is not just in hiring spy runners who have paramilitary experience that the civilian intelligence agencies benefit from a close tie to the military. As a quasimilitary organization itself with a clear command hierarchy, the CIA offers the best products of the military culture enough independence and self-reliance to know when to take the initiative, and sufficient confidence to know when *not* to get out too far ahead of the headquarters element. Many seem to thrive in this environment.

A second factor that has been a good career drawing card for the military to CIA over the years is that intelligence remains a staff function in the armed services. That tends to limit the possibilities for promotion and the number of slots open for military intelligence careers. Furthermore, most officers want to migrate back to line command positions after a tour or two in military intelligence. As a consequence, for those who really like doing intelligence work using paramilitary skills, over time the opportunities are more robust at the CIA or the FBI.

It has long been a bromide in the intelligence world that America's competitive advantage lies in its extraordinary technological competence. As noted earlier, overhead satellite systems may be less important now that we don't have a Soviet missile-test range to monitor in Central Asia. Sigint has also encountered some significant limitations in the proliferation of cheap means of encryption and the spread of fiber optic technology. Nonetheless, the recent flap over warrantless surveillance of domestic phone conversations by the National Security Agency in the wake of 9/11 shows that our technological competence and inventiveness continue to push back at these challenges.

As I understand the media reports on what the NSA proposed to President Bush, it said it could analyze by computer the thousands of telephone calls reportedly emanating from known Al Qaeda communications nodes abroad to American recipients in the United States. By analyzing to whom these calls went and what telephone calls were then spawned by the incoming overseas calls, the NSA hoped to find patterns suggesting terrorist planning or activity. Since the program remains classified, it is hard to tell exactly what the NSA hoped to achieve and what it actually did find, but it appears to be an effort at a kind of data mining made possible by the extraordinary power of the NSA's supercomputers. As events have played out since the outing of this program in late 2005, it seems clear that the American people want to pursue any lead that will help diminish the Al Qaeda threat, but they want some safeguards and accountability for the process as well. Perhaps the FISC can provide that confidence and oversight.

Equally impressive are the SOFLAMs (Special Operations Forces LAser Markers) that Berntsen and the Special Forces teams brought to Afghanistan after 9/11. These laser targeting instruments helped small bands of American paramilitary forces "paint" Taliban targets so that B-52s based in

Diego Garcia, B-1s based near St. Louis, Missouri, and F-18 Hornet aircraft off Persian Gulf–based carriers could blow them to pieces. Without these remarkable technological aids, manned by American paramilitary case officers embedded with Northern Alliance troops in the remotest areas of the Hindu Kush, America's response to the 9/11 horror would have been much slower and more arduous.

A third remarkable technical breakthrough that enabled both airborne reconnaissance in Afghanistan and Iraq and delivery of more firepower was the Predator unmanned aerial vehicle (UAV) developed by the CIA in the mid-nineties. DCI James Woolsey put his name on the line for the development of the Predator, and it has filled an enormous gap in America's overhead reconnaissance and offensive capabilities in tight and remote locations. Stepping up to develop technical espionage tools like this drone is the precise mission of the DCI, now the DNI, as leader of the intelligence community. The U.S Air Force reportedly had been less enthusiastic about it initially, because it removed a pilot from an airborne mission.

Perhaps the greatest need for a technological breakthrough in the spy world, however, is not in the front lines penetrating the terrorist target but in the back rooms, as it were, permitting analysts to shape and get to the heart of the reams of unclassified information pouring in every day from the Middle East and elsewhere. This is joined to an equally great demand for immediate translation of Arabic language documents and Internet communications.

Just as President Reagan was able to grab the Soviets'

attention by announcing his Strategic Defense Initiative to build an antimissile defense system protecting the United States, so a declaration by the United States that it has a technological breakthrough to read terrorist communications on the Internet will convince Al Qaeda that their communications are no longer secure. That's why the CIA's exploration of new spy communications possibilities through its investment several years ago in In-Q-tel, a Silicone Valley investor in new communications technologies, is so clever. It makes the point that we are not standing still in dealing with new espionage challenges, just as the U.S. Army is investing millions to try to protect itself against improvised explosive devices (IED) by getting a jump ahead of the modifications to the technology.

In a perverse way, however, the intelligence community's obsession with secrecy and its technological ability to cut itself off from other governmental, academic, and industrial partners in the pursuit of global jihadist terrorism has impeded its efforts and its successes.

There has been a historic turnover of analysts in the IC since the end of the cold war, but not yet in the tradecraft and communications that permit them to do their jobs. Many bright young analysts coming from universities or the private sector find their abilities to communicate on the job with outside sources of intelligence information on the topics of their expertise circumscribed by office computers that do not talk to anybody outside their employing component or classified milieu. This is absurd in an era when Google and Wikipedia are revolutionizing the way information is gathered, organized, and communicated around the world. It makes no sense when the entity that we are most desirous of penetrating is itself using the Internet and cell phone technology to make its plans and carry out its deadly mission. Finally, it is hopelessly self-limiting and self-defeating at a time when U.S. intelligence no longer has exclusive or proprietary expertise about its principal target, as arguably it might have had on the Soviets until the final days of the USSR. We need all the help we can get in understanding, following, and talking about Al Qaeda, which means we need to be on the open circuits as much as we can. This will be the major hurdle for the CIA and the other intelligence agencies to overcome. Secrecy is not always desirable; "not invented here" is no longer a credible defense; and outreach in the exchange of ideas and information is the best way to access and create the most accurate and comprehensive intelligence reports.

Once again, overprotection of intelligence information and insularity are a misapprehension of the intelligence mission today. We are interested in stopping future terrorist recruitments and attacks, and we need to be out there in the ether of the Internet and World Wide Web, making book on terrorists that will lead to busts.

Chapter Twelve

Foreign Liaison Services and Spying Lawfully

On several occasions during this narrative we have mentioned the role of friendly foreign intelligence liaison services and their importance in helping U.S. intelligence do things indirectly that we could not accomplish alone. As America's humint sources dried up in key venues in the Middle East prior to 9/11, we became more dependent on friendly foreign intelligence services with which we had a formal relationship to fill the gap.

This is not always an advantageous position to be in, as we learned in Afghanistan in the 1980s. In supplying the mujahedin with arms and matériel, we became quite dependent on Pakistan's Inter-Services Intelligence agency (ISI) to act as an intru uu dinry. While supporting the effort to remove the Soviets from control in Afghanistan, ISI wanted to replace them with Islamist Pashtun tribal elements friendly to Pakistan, hence the rise to power of the Taliban.[1] It is obviously a mistake to be dependent on a liaison service for basic day-to-day direction of the mission when there are several contradictory goals at play, especially when our agents do not understand the local language(s) well enough to fully comprehend what is taking place. It is fair to say that after the Soviets' departure from Afghanistan in 1989, followed precipitously by our own drawdown, the CIA was taken for a ride by ISI and the Saudi intelligence service, both of which were pursuing their own agendas.

Formal intelligence liaison relationships between cooperating services are seldom reduced to writing, even between long-term allies. The less said the better is the norm. The relationships go forward on the basis of mutual benefit and back-scratching. When the United States is operating at a linguistic, logistical, and philosophical disadvantage, as it was in Afghanistan in the late 1980s, the liaison arrangement does not work very well. But when it is a case of each service making use of its comparative advantage in a given location to advance an agreed-upon goal, then such an arrangement clearly pays off.

It will be a long time (if ever) before U.S. spy runners will be able to circulate as freely and productively in certain Middle Eastern venues like Iran without drawing attention to themselves, but that inhibition might not affect a German or a Palestinian. If we can use surrogates as our eyes and ears in places where Americans are currently unwelcome, it may be a satisfactory temporary expedient.

However, one area of liaison cooperation that may not continue for much longer is the use of forcible renditions of terrorist suspects to "friendly" services for purposes of interrogation. This represents a new wrinkle on the concept of rendition discussed previously, in which terrorist suspects were snatched and rendered to the custody of U.S. courts for trial. Since 9/11, on several occasions, the CIA has turned over terrorist suspects to friendly Middle Eastern liaison services for incarceration and interrogation on the announced principle that commonality of language and culture would bring better results than if the United States held and questioned them. The unstated premise also appeared to be that these countries would not be constrained to follow the Geneva Conventions Common Article 3 prohibitions against cruel and inhumane treatment in the questioning that followed, although most were queried formally by the United States about their intentions to follow international human rights law and often replied in the affirmative. There has been a growing outcry against this new practice of "extraordinary renditions" and the secret prisons to which certain alleged high-value terrorists have been rendered by the CIA. For that reason I believe the practice has been for the most part discontinued. Where it has not been discontinued, I believe it will shortly be outlawed.

One of the causes for ending the practice is the removal to Syria of Maher Arar from U.S. custody in New York in September 2002. Arar is a dual national of Canada and Syria. He was born in Syria but emigrated to Canada, where he studied computer engineering and information technology at McGill University and became a Canadian citizen. On the basis of erroneous information supplied to U.S. authorities by the government of Canada, Arar was placed on a "watch list" at JFK airport in New York, designating him as Al Qaeda. The derogatory information on Arar was compiled by a unit of the Royal Canadian Mounted Police (RCMP) based on Arar's association with known Al Qaeda suspects in Toronto. A Canadian commission chaired by Justice Dennis O'Connor that investigated the Arar matter on behalf of the Canadian government for over a year found that Arar was mistakenly labeled "Al Qaeda" to U.S. authorities instead of merely "a person of interest" to Canadian intelligence.[2]

On the basis of the erroneous Canadian information, and allegedly because of independent but never revealed information adduced separately by U.S. authorities, Arar was imprisoned by the United States upon disembarking from a flight from Switzerland in September 2002, on his way back to Canada. In the immigration hearing that followed, Arar was found to be a member of Al Qaeda and summarily deported to Syria. Although the flawed intelligence that formed the basis for Arar's removal was supplied by Canada, the Canadian government was neither advised nor consulted about the U.S. decision to remove him to Syria, contrary to normal practice between the two nations.[3] Arar was transported by private jet to Amman, Jordan, and thence to Damascus by road. The Syrian authorities promptly pounced on him, imprisoned him in a cell the size of a coffin, and proceeded to interrogate him and beat him with an electric cable for several weeks. After that, according to Arar, the beatings became less frequent, but he was held in his coffinlike cell for a year until he was released into Canadian custody in October 2003 without ever acknowledging any connection to Al Qaeda. Arar has since moved his family to British Columbia, where he states that he is having trouble finding a job because of the mental anguish inflicted by the Syrians. He has just been awarded a $7 million settlement by the Canadian government and has brought a suit against the U.S. government for reparations.

There are a number of reasons why this case has produced such an outcry in Canada. There is no question that primary responsibility for the flawed intelligence that caused Arar to be removed from the United States is Canadian. In the months after 9/11, the Canadian government was apparently so swamped by the need to process suspicious information about persons crossing back and forth between the United States and Canada that the Royal Canadian Mounted Police, the primary liaison with the American FBI to accomplish this task, had to farm it out to one of its divisions that had no previous experience with the terms on which intelligence information was to be exchanged with the Americans. The caveats and limitations on use to which the Canadian intelligence could be put by the FBI were either not known or not stated by the liaison component, so the flawed info about Arar's status was relied upon by the U.S. immigration judge.[4]

Nonetheless, the consequences of the Canadian mistake would not have been so ghastly if the United States had kept the Canadian side informed on what it intended to do to Arar, and most particularly that he would be removed to Syria with its abysmal human rights record. The Canadians wanted and expected him to be removed to Canada. The consequences of the Arar rendition to Syria have already introduced a noticeable cooling in the relations between the RCMP and their U.S. collaborators on border security.[5] This is not a healthy development for two nations that share a four-thousand-mile border and are each other's principal trading partners. Even after Judge O'Connor's report the United States has refused to remove Arar from the U.S. watch list.

A fruitful long-term intelligence liaison relationship cannot for long be built upon the premise that we shall use others to do the dirty work that we are unwilling to do (and reluctant to admit to). Either the cooperating service will be humiliated by international public opinion into discontinuing the practice, as seems to be happening with the new style of renditions, or it will be made unlawful for the United States to do indirectly what its own laws and international law prohibits it from doing directly, in the same way that the Executive Order 12333 currently prohibits political assassinations.

In any event, in the context of the war on terrorism, there exists today a great deal of cooperation between intelligence services confronting similar problems, such as the worldwide movement of Islamist radicals espousing martyrdom or suicidal terrorism, despite the objectionable practice of extraordinary renditions. Even nations whose leaders propose different philosophical approaches to the problem find that their intelligence services cooperate fully and rapidly with one another on practical questions of information sharing on identities and evidence. That is why admission to the inner circle of intelligence liaisons has been opened to law enforcement worldwide, for the forensic support it supplied that enabled the London police to identify the perpetrators of the July 7, 2005, London Underground attacks in several days. Tight cooperation between friendly intelligence liaison services and their law enforcement partners represents the most effective counterterrorist force that can be mounted against today's Islamist suicide bombers.

Among the many distasteful issues raised by the practices of extraordinary rendition and coercive interrogations is the question whether there is a proper or at least internationally accepted concept of spying. In a profession that is by definition unlawful—i.e., stealing another country's secrets—how can it be possible to spy with propriety? Isn't that oxymoronic? The distinction seems to be that while the United States recognizes that its espionage breaks the laws of other countries, it is committed to acting lawfully and properly *within* the United States. Spies are not supposed to violate U.S. law. That is why there was such consternation over Seymour Hersh's revelation of the "family jewels" in 1974 and the warrantless domestic surveillance in 2005 and 2006. As Vice President Cheney and former defense secretary Donald Rumsfeld are fond of noting, the world is a dangerous place. Espionage in defense of the United States in order to prevent another 9/11-style attack is a practice that if not countenanced explicitly by international law has existed since the dawn of civilization—the second oldest profession, some would argue. But we do not wish to undermine our domestic legal system and constitutional order by spying on

U.S. citizens at home or abroad without judicial sanction or congressional oversight.

Thus, when pursuant to presidential direction the CIA engages in questionable practices, such as torture or coercive interrogations in secret prisons overseas, using techniques that constitute "cruel and inhumane treatment" of prisoners in violation of U.S. and international law, serious questions are raised of legality and propriety. The U.S. Supreme Court so ruled in the summer of 2006 in the case of *Hamdan v. Rumsfeld,* and the Congress followed the Court's ruling in passing the Military Commissions Act of 2006. Under *Hamdan* and the MCA, unlawful combatant detainees of the U.S. military held in Department of Defense custody must be afforded the protections of Article 3 of the Geneva Conventions prohibiting "cruel and inhumane treatment." There is still some question as to whether the strictures of *Hamdan* and the MCA apply to non-Defense agencies such as the CIA holding unlawful combatants in secret prisons, but the MCA's sponsors believe it does, and the international climate affecting cooperation with U.S. intelligence on this issue is fast deteriorating.[6]

The concern for propriety doesn't begin—or stop—there. The CIA and the KGB reached informal agreement during the cold war that neither service would target members of the other for assassination. It was perhaps the unheard-of manifestation of honor among thieves in the spy world. Furthermore, both CIA and the KGB were committed morally and contractually to honor their commitments to pay agents or their families if the agents were jailed or executed. The terms of this devil's bargain were to be honored irrespective of its legal unenforceability.

There are also many issues that need to be resolved respecting the CIA's use of "dirty assets." As touched upon previously, it would constitute a problem for an American case officer to intentionally engage as a spy someone who had, for example, knowingly participated in a plot to kill U.S. persons or who had actually performed such a deed. Under current law and practice, the CIA would have to file a crimes report with the U.S. Department of Justice before going forward with such an agent recruitment. Technically, the Justice Department could turn the CIA down, and the DCI (now probably the DNI) would have to fight it out with the attorney general before the president, if the CIA wished to proceed.

Is this the customary practice that awaits a newly reinvigorated CIA charged with preempting and preventing future terrorist attacks against the United States, or a recipe for a bureaucratic power struggle? What is FBI procedure in recruiting an informant in the Mob who may have participated in killing U.S. citizens or other criminal acts? Can it be done, and with what safeguards? In my view, in an age of jihadist terror, the CIA will need flexibility in working with assets who have blood on their hands, subject to regular review by Justice and the congressional oversight committees, but in a manner that permits the CIA to use its judgment and act expeditiously when the need for intelligence to prevent a terrorist act is great.

Likewise, I have never found the issue of warrantless surveillance to be unresolvable. The direction in which the Congress currently appears to be going makes sense to me, especially in light of a recent lower federal court decision finding the present practice unconstitutional. As the U.S. attorney general's January 17, 2007, letter to Congress seems to suggest, the Foreign Intelligence Surveillance Court should be directed to ride herd on the NSA program and brief the oversight committees regularly. Confidence must be reestablished that the spy agencies can be trusted to do their jobs competently and soberly, given credible oversight, because we need them to gain the information about terrorist planning in this country. That is, after all, the thrust of the president's order to preempt or prevent future 9/11s.

As to secret prisons and ghost detainees, I believe the prisons should be dismantled along with Guantánamo. The detainees should be held as "unlawful combatants" if they meet the criteria established by the U.S. Supreme Court after *Hamdi* and *Hamdan* and tried for war crimes pursuant to the procedure established in the MCA. Coercive interrogations for all detainees, in violation of Common Article 3 of the 1949 Geneva Conventions, should be flatly discontinued. As the Canadians, the Italians, and the Germans have recently reminded us, the damage done to America's reputation far exceeds the value of the intelligence information gained when it comes by illegal means. In all likelihood, as the FBI has argued, more successful interrogations over an admittedly longer period of time result from positive reinforcements and gaining the confidence of the subject than from torture or the threat of it.

A final word about the ticking bomb scenario and torture warrants, as favored by Harvard law professor Alan

Dershowitz. As Professor David Luban has written in an excellent article published in September 2005, the frequency of genuine ticking bomb situations may be vastly overstated.[7] In the rare instances when they occur or appear to be taking place, interrogators will seek the information by any means at hand and throw themselves on the mercy of the court afterward. Few prosecutors will try, and fewer juries will convict, if the immediate nature of the danger exists or is perceived in good faith to have existed. There is also the unpleasant bureaucratic fact that it will be the ordinary case officers in the field who pay the price for these excesses. The CIA officers allegedly involved in the Milan and Macedonia snatchings described in Chapter 10 may never be found to receive the subpoenas issued for them to appear, but they will also never be able to return to Italy or Germany without facing legal process.

In sum, too much is at stake for U.S. spy agencies to violate U.S. or international law in the pursuit of terrorists. This is what Islamist radicals want. Their tactic is to get the West, and the United States in particular, to abandon the norms of civilization and lawful behavior and get down in the gutter with them. We must resist that temptation.

Chapter Thirteen

Updating Operational and
Analytical Tradecraft

One of espionage's greatest challenges today is modernizing its approach to gathering and analyzing intelligence information. This problem exists beyond the issues of harnessing new information technology, managing vast amounts of open source information, and acquiring the cheap encryption technology discussed previously.

On the collection side, America's spy handlers will not be successful in spotting, assessing, developing, and recruiting terrorist assets from the protected vantage point of official U.S. installations abroad–embassies, military bases, consulates, etc. Aside from the fact that for security reasons U.S. facilities are as forbidding and seemingly impenetrable as Fort

Knox these days, the cast of characters one is likely to have reason to meet from an official U.S. position is not the one from which terrorists or their friends is likely to be drawn. Far more promising for purposes of infiltrating Islamist terrorist movements are those nongovernmental activities that offer commercial, medical, spiritual, educational, or practical help to a Middle Eastern populace that is poorly led and poorly provided for. That will be particularly difficult after America's involvement in the war in Iraq.

By any measure, this will be a tough assignment, both to construct and to carry out, and will demand unquestionable competence in Arabic or a local dialect, and a knowledge of the totems and lore of the region. That is why it will not be possible to create an army of capable nonofficial cover (NOC) spies in a hurry.

As noted above, I do not believe NOC possibilities can be created on a wholesale basis. If they are to work, the candidate must be a remarkably independent, self-reliant officer who does not require a lot of hand-holding. Otherwise, as has too often been the case in the past, the care and feeding of NOC officers by inside spy runners takes up too much support time by other case officers and is not productive overall.

Furthermore, nonofficial cover officers will have difficulty bringing spouses and family members to many high-priority intelligence postings because of the dangerous environment that caused the United States to build maximum-security embassies in the first place. This will clearly be an endeavor where many may be called but few chosen. In the majority of cases, it is a far more difficult calling than that practiced by the cold war generation of spy runners. It is a wholly different situation when a breakdown in cover can result in prison or summary execution, as contrasted with diplomatic expulsion as a persona non grata.

It is also the reason that there must be a widely understood and favorable resolution of the Valerie Plame Wilson outing so that future potential overseas operatives can be reassured that with the myriad practical cover problems they face, their own government's determination to protect their cover is *not* one of them. Sadly, I believe the conviction of Vice President Cheney's chief of staff, I. Lewis Libby, for perjury and obstruction of justice has not made that important point. The significant harm done to Ms. Wilson's contacts and friends, and to the expenditure of time, effort, and funds by Ms. Wilson and the U.S. government in order to establish her cover, a cover that by all accounts she worked hard and successfully to maintain, has been undercut by the anomaly that neither the admitted leaker of her name, former deputy secretary of state Richard Armitage, nor the reporter of the leak, Robert Novak, has been charged or punished for the offense.

That will mean, as a practical matter, that the principal burden of the espionage effort against the terrorist target will continue to fall to case officers working with friendly foreign intelligence liaison services, probably in concert with local law enforcement and the FBI. There is much to be gained in this arrangement, especially over the near term, but the limitations are also clear. In working through intermediaries, one is often constrained to take the second sip from the cup or see events through the eyes of others. As we learned in

Afghanistan in the 1980s, one can never be certain that one is getting *all* the information, or getting it in an unfiltered form. Nonetheless, the CIA and the FBI have a great deal to bring to the bargain in terms of gadgetry, know-how, and resources for our friends—and if we have a solid understanding of the target country, it may work out for a time.

It may also be the best we can do on the humint side until we decide to go all out to recruit our own indigenous sources of Middle Eastern cultural and linguistic knowledge—Arab Americans. It is catastrophic that first- and second-generation U.S. citizens of Arab American ancestry are being denied clearances to work in the intelligence world because they may still have a close relative resident in the Middle East. It's the *Korematsu* discrimination case of World War II all over again. That's the U.S. Supreme Court decision in which American citizens of Japanese ancestry were summarily removed from their homes on the West Coast and imprisoned in "camps" in the Midwest during the war, on the theory that they were a dangerous potential "fifth column" of opposition to the American government. Luckily, it appears that the new director of national intelligence, Admiral Mike McConnell, believes that the United States is missing a golden opportunity here, and it has been reported that he intends to go full bore to try to hire Arab Americans with language and culture skills throughout the intelligence community.

The reader can plainly see where I am headed with this line of argument. More money and more spy runners are not by themselves the solution to our humint spying deficit against Islamist terrorism. Obvious as it may sound, it's the people argument again. I should prefer smaller numbers of trained and capable case officers to platoons of new recruits. In this ticklish equation, it's the *quality* of the personnel that counts for success. In that regard, it is interesting to note CIA director Michael Hayden's take on the subject. According to his remarks on C-SPAN's *Q&A* program on April 14, 2007, his biggest challenge, he says, is absorbing all the newly hired analysts and case officers brought on board since 9/11. He further declared that 50 percent of the CIA has been hired since September 11, 2001, and one fifth of the agency's analysts have been hired since April 2006. That is a shocking set of statistics.[1]

The analytical side of intelligence work against Islamist terrorism also cries out for reform. The explosion of open source information has already been discussed. Even harder to improve than the management of this torrent, however, may be the need to change the *deployment* of analytical resources. For purposes of preventing the next terrorist attack against the United States, it makes no sense to concentrate all our analytical brainpower on current intelligence to the exclusion of looking down the road to see what we may be facing next. That is the essence of warnings intelligence. It was the reason why the Board of National Estimate was reconstituted by DCI general Walter Bedell Smith in 1950. Estimative intelligence—making reasoned prognostications on future developments—was an OSS innovation during World War II, and it was abandoned for a time when OSS was disbanded in 1945. Most of the criticisms of the analytical work done by the IC on Iraqi WMD in 2002 and the run-up to 9/11 have dwelled on the extent to which analytical resources were tied up on current intelligence issues. The effort to keep the president and members of Congress informed about happenings all over the world consumes vast amounts of personal and fiscal resources, often without a great deal of value added over the news broadcast simultaneously by CNN. Most of the criticisms were focused then on the need for the new DNI to devote substantial resources to trying to figure out more accurately, and in a more timely fashion, the threats the United States will face in the future, not only in political terms, but on existential or resource issues such as water, overpopulation, and disease.

It has always shocked my conscience that after having missed the Khomeini revolution in Iran in 1979, the intelligence community did not learn its lesson and devote sufficient analytical resources to the rise and growth of Islamist fundamentalism. Apparently there was a significant national intelligence estimate on the subject in 1995, but not much in addition since. The growth of Osama bin Laden and his ideology is just the sort of phenomenon that intelligence should have been focusing on, for its potential tendency to grow and to spread. Yet apart from Mike Scheuer's unit in the Directorate of Operations following bin Laden's personal activities, we seem to have been largely unaware of the explosive nature of his credo and how it might metastasize, until late in the day.

This leads to a more pertinent and practical point. Analysts should not simply advance because they publish in the President's Daily Brief. They should not just be rewarded for good current intelligence analysis. They should take the time to think about and write on matters *before* they hit the headlines. The essence of good intelligence analysis is to identify the germs before they become pandemics. As in any intelligence culture smitten with present threats and deployed for two-year assignments, the IC has clearly not been developing the long-term expertise to follow a given development from seedling to forest.

None of this is either new or surprising. As noted, it was remarked on in all the post-9/11 critiques. In the big bureaucracy that the IC has become, personal responsibility for mastering an intelligence account and sticking with it has been the forte of the smaller intelligence outfits in Washington, such as the Bureau of Intelligence and Research (INR) at State, rather than the bigger Directorate of Intelligence at CIA where much of U.S. finished intelligence used to be written. In addition, the creation of a genuine information-sharing environment, laughed at earlier as a wish rather than a command, will take a number of years to bring about fully. It is difficult to change lifelong habits built on the hard realities of protecting sources in law enforcement and espionage. Nonetheless, there was hope that with Ambassador John Negroponte taking the helm as DNI, an officer who had had a careerlong exposure to intelligence and policy making, the IC would be off to a good start. Instead, he departed after only twenty-two months on the job. One is tempted to conclude that Ambassador Negroponte discovered what many critics of the Intelligence Reform and Terrorism Prevention Act of 2004 had already sadly observed, that in terms of executive authority the DNI was little more than the old chief of the intelligence community staff with a few more medals and epaulets.

Nevertheless, part of the DNI's responsibility as CEO of the IC must mean that the president and Congress will look to him for valid long-term estimates, and that he will focus on the stuff of tomorrow's challenges. The president must make it clear that this is what he expects from his intelligence community.

Part Four

Why Spy?
Should We Do It?

Chapter Fourteen

A Spy for the
Twenty-first Century

A s with many of our nation's problems, espionage in the twenty-first century boils down to the issues of people, leadership resources, and time. Let's examine them in order.

All available evidence suggests that the events of September 11 have unleashed a mammoth wave of renewed interest in espionage by patriotic Americans, although it is unclear whether the new recruits know what they are signing up for. It's also probably accurate that the spymasters at Langley and in the DNI's office aren't completely certain how to channel this new torrent of volunteers—or are learning as the war on terrorism continues to unfold. It was reported in 2006 that the CIA alone was looking at one thousand résumés a month!

Apart from the difficulty of carefully processing so many applications, the issue is, what should the national humint authority be looking for? How many? And with what qualifications? And at what ages? And to fill what positions? These are all obvious questions for a career service. Yet if one does not fully comprehend the nature of the espionage puzzle one is trying to solve, the answers to these questions are often difficult to discern.

As noted above, proficiency in hard languages (or the ability to acquire them) and cultural awareness are a given, and I would hope nonnegotiable. Maturity, self-reliance, and independence of judgment are critical if we shall be assigning these officers to be our outriders in distant and hostile environments. But what is the proper balance between inside officers, perhaps in liaison with friendly intelligence services, and nonofficial cover types who, like the Soviet illegals of the 1930s, may be asked to build their cover and lie low for a considerable period of time before becoming operational? The DNI and DCIA can't possibly yet know the full answers to these questions. So what good does it do if we recruit a team of all-star spy runners and we have no career plan for their services? It has always been my view that mediocrity can never recruit, train, and hold on to highfliers—and I am concerned that after the emptying out of Langley during the 1990s, and more recently under Porter Goss, the CIA is not well situated to exploit the windfall of new talent that might currently be knocking on its door. It might be able to attract them, but can it appropriately train and hold them?

My strongest recommendation is that the DNI and DCIA

concentrate their human resources efforts on figuring out how to quickly train, utilize, and retain this burst of new hires who will be needed if meaningful penetrations of Islamist terrorist groups are to be achieved. It will be hard to do, but reengineering the can-do spirit and family feeling of the old DO (often mistakenly criticized as the camaraderie of the "old boy network" before it was corrupted by careerism in the late 1980s) is what I am referring to. As DCI Richard Helms (1966–73) often argued, we are an honorable tribe, we spies, working toward what's best for our country, and the high ideals and morals of that quest have never been more needed against an enemy that shows none. "Elitism" has acquired a hideous reputation these days because, at the CIA at any rate, it was wrapped up with the alleged Ivy League and Wall Street origins of the place. But a skilled intelligence operational elite is exactly what the CIA should be looking for and trying to build. If your organization doesn't foster and reward the grit and esprit de corps that will get you through the dangers and sacrifices of this difficult profession, in my view, you won't recruit and keep the high-caliber spy runner we are after.

It's also important to tap a steady stream of new talents beyond those who may excel at exploiting the seven motivations for espionage. Military officers have already been mentioned, for those occasions where paramilitary skills are critical, such as in future Afghanistans. But I would add an additional category, and not a new one, that will be able to exploit the growing interdependence of intelligence and law enforcement. The CIA was founded by lawyers—Donovan, Dulles, Wisner, Des Fitzgerald, Karamessines, and Colby—and the particular sensitivity they brought to issues of process and propriety remains important, despite the fact that the espionage mission requires breaking the laws of foreign countries.

To continue to be most effective in the war on terrorism, the cross assigning of officers with different backgrounds to the NCTC remains a priority, because the assigned officers develop a broader understanding of detecting and countering terrorist activity in a variety of different situations.

The bottom line, however, is quality, not quantity. I favor a clandestine service that is sized at somewhere between the projected 50 percent increase in the number of case officers and current onboard strength. It is better to start slowly, paying attention to training, career planning, and experience, than to flood the organization with indigestible numbers of new recruits.

For realization of the above, the quality of leadership is critical. I am principally referring to the role of the national humint director, who is the director of the Central Intelligence Agency, and the deputy director for operations in that organization. But it extends far beyond these two. Meaningful leadership for a rebirth of U.S. espionage must be a priority of the DNI, the president, and the Congress as well. More broadly, it dovetails into a greater call for national service generally in the United States. To understand this larger requirement one must step back a bit into cold war history.

One of the strongest determinants of U.S. spying success during the cold war was the position of the United States as the principal counterweight to Joseph Stalin's push for dominance in Europe, and eventually all over the world, after

World War II. (Tony Judt's brilliant new book makes that plain.[1]) To counter the expansion of the Soviet empire, our European allies asked us to maintain a European presence after World War II through support for the creation of a West German state and the deutsche mark to stabilize it. The United States responded further in 1948 with a massive program of financial assistance to Western Europe with the Marshall Plan, and also answered Europe's call for a military alliance with the creation of the North Atlantic Treaty Organization (NATO). In what became a U.S. policy of containment of Soviet expansion after George Kennan's prescient "long telegram" from Moscow in 1947, the CIA played a leading role. So, over time, in the eyes of much of the free world and behind the Iron Curtain as well, the United States was much admired. Potential spies responded to CIA blandishments not necessarily because they knew much about us or our civilization and values, but because we were willing to stand up to communist imperial expansion. Without really asking for it, the United States had taken over a world leadership role that, among other things, benefited us greatly in espionage recruitments with access to the answers to questions that were important to U.S. national security.

That situation no longer obtains today in the Middle East, where there is the greatest risk of attack. The "good guy" factor is no longer operative in our favor. On the contrary, anti-Americanism is on the rise all over the world, but particularly in the region that is most important to us due to our economic dependence on oil. Arab-based TV stations Al-Jazeera and Al-Arabia are constantly showing grisly pictures of Arab families being shot, maimed, and destroyed in countless daily battles in Iraq or Lebanon or Gaza, and the constant theme is that this is the fault of the Americans or their clients, the Israelis. The leadership in Egypt or Saudi Arabia or Jordan or Pakistan may have different and longer perspectives on America's role in the Middle East, but the millions of young people under twenty in these countries, undereducated, underskilled, and without jobs, money, or prospects are thrown back on the mosques and radical Islam for their sustenance. They are imbibing large doses of anti-Americanism from Hezbollah, Hamas, and the daily news broadcasts showing suicide bombings and death in Iraq, Lebanon, and Gaza.

So American espionage will have its work cut out for it. Already challenged by diminished experience, weak linguistic skills, and meager cultural knowledge of Islam and the region, this virulent opposition to the United States and what it is perceived to stand for will hinder easy spy recruitments for the moment at least.

That is one of the clearest reasons I can think of why leadership and support at the agency and national levels for the espionage mission remains vital. The estrangement of the CIA spies from the White House over Iraq that started before the 2004 presidential election, and continued during the tenure of DCI Porter Goss, must be brought to an end. In that connection, presidential leadership does not consist of badgering intelligence analysts to arrive at conclusions that in their view the intelligence data will not support. Further, it is not enhanced by a National Security Council or Department of Defense giving greater credence to information being supplied unilaterally by émigrés with axes to grind than might be the case if the IC were allowed to vet that information against its own expertise.

Spy runners need to know that the president and Congress fully support very difficult assignments to penetrate Islamist terrorist groups. Agency leadership must emphasize that today's espionage mission is a lot tougher than cold war spying, and it will take time to prepare to do it successfully.

In addition to the issues of people and leadership, successful espionage in the twenty-first century will depend upon adequate resources and the time to deploy these resources. The intelligence community budget for FY 2007 is continually projected by media reports to be in the range of $50 billion. Of that amount, about 80 percent is spent by the Department of Defense on signals and overhead reconnaissance hardware, and on defense-related intelligence gathering and analysis. In anybody's eyes these are big numbers. It will pay a lot of spies and analysts and build a heap of spy gear. The question in my mind, however, is whether it is pouring money into the appropriate pots to fully enhance U.S. spying.

I believe the national interest would be best served by an increase in manpower for the clandestine service with an emphasis on quality, hiring for the long term, and not moving before the DCIA and DNI figure out what to do with the new recruits.

On the issue of hard-language training, the U.S. government has to take a more catholic, indeed *global* view. I am aware that recent intelligence authorization bills in the Congress have beefed up the language study account for the spy services, but this issue is far broader than America's intelligence needs. As noted earlier, in the aftermath of the Soviet *Sputnik 1* launch in 1957, the U.S. Congress enacted the National Defense Education Act (NDEA). The NDEA represented a national judgment and commitment that serious steps needed to be taken to improve U.S. competencies in those areas relating to the challenges of a wider world. The NDEA is no longer funded to meet today's challenges, which are not limited to the needs of U.S. intelligence gathering and analysis. The NDEA ought to be reexamined in the light of this new *Sputnik*-like challenge, and funded appropriately to counter the spread of Islamist jihadism in broader ways.

Part of the national leadership role on intelligence addressed above suggests that the president ought to open a dialogue with the American people on what it will take to successfully combat the threat of Islamist terrorism now before us. If it remains U.S. policy that future 9/11s must be preempted or prevented, the responsibility to accomplish these goals goes well beyond military engagement and the roles of law enforcement and intelligence. As a nation, we need to know much more about what we are up against strategically since we can't fight this threat effectively on an incident-by-incident basis. In many quarters, the notion of a global war on terrorism has the ring of a political campaign slogan rather than an agreed-upon agenda with specific milestones. The notion of a "long war" may capture best what we are involved in (although the term has since been suppressed by the administration), if by that is meant an analogy to the cold war, where we learned to live with the possibility of a nuclear exchange for over forty years while we tried to understand and overcome the communist forces arrayed against us.

To me there are three phenomena encompassed in the current threat of Islamist terrorism that are quite disturbing.

The first is the concept of "martyrdom." It is the idea of suicidal attack that makes the war on terrorism a formidable threat psychologically as well as physically. Unless one is prepared to encase the entire American way of life in an all-pervasive blanket of security—a task too formidable and too dismissive of most human freedoms to contemplate—one can never fully protect oneself from the threat of a suicide attacker.

The second is the corruption of jihadism in Islam that encourages martyrdom under current circumstances in Iraq, Palestine, Indonesia, and Afghanistan to achieve political goals. To me this constant effort to find ways to destroy human life, on a sectarian basis currently in Iraq and Afghanistan, and against Israel by Hamas and Hezbollah in Gaza and Lebanon, is hard to square with the tenets of one of the world's three great monotheistic religions. Even without an episcopal hierarchy in Islam, I have been startled that few if any significant imams have stepped forward to condemn suicide bombing masquerading as martyrdom. I understand that this is partially due to the corruption of the concept of *takfir,* by which the martyrdom group is denouncing the reluctant imams as apostates, but it is obviously a much greater dilemma for the world if we stand on the threshold of a holy war.

Lastly, the proliferation of failed states serving as sanctuaries for Islamist terrorists is disquieting. Iraq, Afghanistan, Somalia, now perhaps Lebanon, and eventually perhaps

Palestine are all frightening harbingers of what the war on terrorism may be leading to.

These phenomena argue for a more strategic and long-term approach to the spreading challenge of Islamist terrorism than simply year-by-year increases in the intelligence, law enforcement, and defense budgets. Nonetheless, it is imperative that we keep investing in research to seek technological assistance to help solve our intelligence collection and analytical problems, so we can know more about what we are up against. For the policy maker the choice is not between humint and technical collection, but toward a mixture of both that most enhances accomplishment of the mission. Recall that President Dwight Eisenhower continued to fund the early tests of overhead reconnaissance satellites in the late 1950s despite many disappointing, unsuccessful launches of the Corona satellite system. We need to find a way to shrink the mountain of intelligence information that analysts must be conversant with and pore through every day to stay ahead of terrorist threats.

Finally, there are the all-important questions of priorities and time. *We needed solutions yesterday* to the intelligence and law enforcement problems surrounding the prevention of future terrorist acts—more linguists, more experienced and knowledgeable analysts, more and better control of intelligence information, more technology, and more capable spies—but unfortunately real progress always takes time, and it will take experience. It is disquieting to observe that over 50 percent of the CIA's analysts and case officers have been hired in the past five years. While we are putting the blocks in place for the future, and learning how to combat and prevent terrorism, it is most unhelpful to lose patience with the efforts of analysts, spy runners, and law enforcement for a seeming failure to understand and make progress toward preempting all future terrorist acts today. By going to the open market to hire contractors to fill short-term gaps, we may be undercutting the likelihood of growing professionalism and expertise from within. Contractors should only be a short-term palliative— not a permanent solution. It causes me to shiver when I understand that the desk officer for Japan in the DO comes from the outside, and is in fact an employee of a non-USG entity. What are the security and chain-of-command ramifications of that situation? Unless we are to make a police state of our country (and probably not even then), we shall always run some risk of terrorist attack, especially if the attractiveness of suicide or martyrdom operations remains a reality. The only thing we should insist upon is that law enforcement and the intelligence community are making a solid effort to move forward—and the best indicator of that effort may be that they are in constant communication with one another and are sharing the necessary intelligence information.

Conclusion

Can We Make Espionage Work in the Twenty-first Century?

If the popular response in the United States to the 9/11 attacks is any guide, there *is* support in our country for doing whatever is necessary to prevent future terrorist attacks. This includes upgrading and improving espionage efforts to penetrate terrorist cells and work with friendly foreign intelligence services to that end. It is often remarked that most Americans don't know much about spying, and probably don't want to know how the mission is accomplished, but if it's a question of homeland security they appear to be all for it. This support also extends to meshing more completely the overlapping roles of spy runners, law enforcement, and the military to fight terrorism. Islamist terrorism is a far greater challenge to

U.S. intelligence in terms of penetrating hostile terrorist cells than the cold war. Instead of trench coats and brush passes, we are fighting an asymmetrical struggle, where much of our technological and traditional war, crime fighting, and spying expertise has been neutralized or altered. The United States and our allies are involved in a vast new learning curve.

American case officers are not yet fully cognizant of the many ways in which the ingrained lessons of the seven principal motivations for espionage will have to be modified to work effectively against the terrorist target. And if the modus operandi of Islamist terror remains jihadist martyrdom operations by nonstate actors from the sanctuary of failed states, the challenge *is* a significant one. It will take a strategically targeted, cross-cutting effort to win the war on terrorism with high-caliber personnel who may endure long waits in the wings before emerging onstage to interrupt the murderous play of a terrorist attack about to unfold. Our leaders need to talk to us about this challenge, for the way to meet it is not just in the realm of better and more successful espionage, law enforcement, and military reactions. It is societal in the broadest sense. The conditions giving rise to the alienation, desperation, and sense of victimhood behind the rise of Islamist terrorism internationally are not matters that can be dealt with by spies, cops, and soldiers alone. Israel-Palestine, oil, and the rise of Shiite nationalism are just several of the overarching issues that must be dealt with comprehensively by our government, our allies, and the United Nations.

That said, Western civilization has no choice but to confront these issues. The challenge of suicidal Islamist extremism must be faced and met—realistically and with a broad team approach. The seven principal motivations for espionage will surely have their place in the struggle. In the end, the possibility of progress and greater prosperity brought about by a globalized economy and more personal freedom will trump a philosophy based on hate, suicide, and destruction.

However, that case has not yet been made satisfactorily.

Is U.S. intelligence up to the challenge of twenty-first-century espionage? My answer is a qualified "yes," if we cope successfully with four important concerns.

First, if the national humint authority—the CIA, or whatever it becomes—cannot reshape, reinvigorate, and remotivate the intelligence bureaucracy, there will not be much chance of succeeding in dealing with the people, leadership, and resource challenges mentioned earlier. The gelatinous, paper-dependent, "not invented here," unimaginative bureaucracy that I encountered in the 1990s at Langley will stifle any new initiatives the DNI or DCIA may be talking about. Spying needs to get back to the highly disciplined, internally motivated, "mom-and-pop" store familiarity that I remember from the 1960s. It needs to be more nimble and entrepreneurial. Second, and flowing from the first, intelligence collection and analysis must be extricated from the pressures of partisan politics to the greatest degree possible. President George W. Bush made the point that the tenure of a DCI did not depend on the party in power but on the merits of the individual when he retained George Tenet as DCI in 2000. Yet he seemed to have forgotten that point in naming Porter Goss as Tenet's successor in 2004. Much appears to have changed since those early days, and intelligence has become a partisan issue. This will have to stop if we expect to get back to objective intelligence collection and analysis.

Third, the role of law enforcement in meeting the challenge of Islamist terrorism really involves two distinct approaches, much like the difference between classic agent spying operations and covert action that CIA case officers practiced for over fifty years. On the one hand, there is the criminal investigative role as the FBI has traditionally pursued it, but the targets are terrorists as opposed to the Mob. The second role is where the bureau embarks on new territory. This is domestic intelligence gathering and analysis akin to MI-5's mission in the UK. It is not fair to say, as some of its critics do, that the bureau has no experience in this domestic intelligence responsibility. It successfully ran overseas collection operations during World War II in Latin America that the CIA took over in 1947. It also penetrated the Communist Party of the United States (CPUSA) thoroughly in the late 1940s, and continued to do so until the CPUSA probably had more FBI undercover agents in its ranks than it did real communists.

I believe it is too early to conclude, as some important observers apparently have, that the FBI cannot perform its domestic intelligence role competently. Congress and the executive branch will have to monitor carefully the FBI's success in creating a domestic intelligence career service to gauge whether or not the bureau's law-enforcement culture can be modified to adopt an MI-5 competence. I believe it will, as these cross-cutting responsibilities like the NCTC gather importance and effectiveness, but the jury is still out.

Finally, it is difficult to overstate the importance to successful reinvigoration of the intelligence community of the role to be played by the congressional intelligence oversight committees, the House Permanent Select Committee on Intelligence and the Senate Select Committee on Intelligence. The Congress considers itself a rightful and critical consumer of intelligence information—as important to the workings of any U.S. government response to terrorist attack as the president. It has the primary responsibility to authorize and appropriate funds for the spies, and its judgments about how well that money is being spent are now at the heart of the constitutional scheme for national security.

In that regard, it is pleasing to note that House speaker Nancy Pelosi has just created a new joint commission composed both of members of the House intelligence committee and senior members of the House appropriations committee to see if the intelligence budget can be both authorized and appropriated by a single committee in the U.S. House of Representatives, as the 9/11 Commission recommended. If that approach works, perhaps the Senate will follow suit.

Insofar as Congress plays politics with its oversight, or neglects rigorous nonpartisan examination of the IC's performance, it weakens the system of checks and balances on which good intelligence depends. One of the clearest examples of the House and Senate intelligence committees' dereliction of their duties in this regard has been the failure to recognize the extent to which the CIA's humint collection and analytical capabilities had atrophied during the transition after the end of the cold war in 1991. As Osama bin Laden and

Islamist terrorism became of greater significance at the end of the twentieth century, the Congress should have joined its voice to that of the DCI, George Tenet, and urged that more be done to enhance the CIA's preparedness to fight this fight. Congress's role is not simply that of consumer and commentator on intelligence, but also that of taskmaster, critic, and enabler. After all, it holds the purse strings.

Notes

INTRODUCTION

1. The terms "spy handler," "spy runner," and "case officer" will be used interchangeably in this text. They refer to the intelligence operations officer, in the CIA or otherwise, whose job it is to recruit and run spies overseas to collect intelligence information on behalf of the United States. This is what most intelligence officers do: They run spies. They seldom actually steal the secrets themselves.

1. ESPIONAGE VERSUS INTELLIGENCE

1. U.S. intelligence calls this "tradecraft," which is itself a euphemism for measures designed to maintain operational security.

2. Kim Philby, *My Silent War* (New York: Grove Press, 1968), p. 49, quoted in Frederick P. Hitz, *The Great Game* (New York: Knopf, 2004), p. 3.

3. *The Great Game,* ibid., p. 182.

4. The workings of the U.S. intelligence community have been one

of Washington's most enduring mysteries. Split as it is between military and civilian tool and chain of command, it has often been a band of warring fiefdoms. Hopefully, the creation of a director of national intelligence in 2004 may alter the reality of this perception.

2. IDEOLOGICAL COMMITMENT

1. Roland Perry, *Last of the Cold War Spies* (New York: Da Capo Press, 2005).

2. Details of Kuklinski's career as a U.S. spy come from Benjamin Weiser's excellent biography, *A Secret Life* (New York: Public Affairs, 2004). The interpretations are mine.

3. The Tolkachev story was related in an excellent article entitled "Tolkachev, a Worthy Successor to Penkovsky" by retired CIA operations officer Barry G. Royden in an unclassified article he wrote in 2003 in *Studies in Intelligence,* a CIA publication that can be found on the Web page of the Center for the Study of Intelligence at https://www.cia.gov/ library/center-for-the-study-of-intelligence/csi-publications.

4. Viktor Cherkashin, *Spy Handler* (New York: Basic Books, 2005), pp. 28, 310.

3. MONEY AND TREASURE

1. Viktor Cherkashin, *Spy Handler* (New York: Basic Books, 2005), p. 29.

2. Actor Chris Cooper captures some of this in his excellent portrayal of Robert Hanssen in the 2007 feature film *Breach* about Hanssen's betrayal.

3. Duane Clarridge, *A Spy for All Seasons* (New York: Scribner, 1998), p. 142ff.

4. REVENGE AND SCORE SETTLING

1. Author's interview with Dr. David Charney, May 7, 2002.

5. SEX, INTIMIDATION, AND BLACKMAIL

1. An "illegal" is a spy with a fictitious name and life history operating without diplomatic protection overseas. The Soviet intelligence services made great use of illegals from their earliest days, often using them as recruiters, couriers, or "sleeper" agents to provide early warning of a possible attack on the USSR.

6. SPYING FOR REASONS OF FRIENDSHIP OR ETHNIC OR RELIGIOUS SOLIDARITY

1. Ruth Marcus, "Accused Spy Used Hong Kong Banks," *Washington Post,* Nov. 28, 1985.

2. U.S. Senate, Subcommittee on Department of Justice Oversight, "Report on the Government's Handling of the Investigation and Prosecution of Dr. Wen Ho Lee." December 20, 2001. Washington: Government Printing Office, 2001.

7. THE SPY GAME FOR THE SAKE OF THE GAME

1. James Srodes, *Allen Dulles: Master of Spies* (Washington: Regnery, 1999), p. 227.

8. INTELLIGENCE FAILURES AND POLITICIZATION

1. Richard A. Posner, *Preventing Surprise Attacks: Intelligence Reform in the Wake of 9/11* (Lanham, Md.: Rowan and Littlefield 2005).

2. Roberta Wohlstetter, *Pearl Harbor: Warning and Decision* (Palo Alto, Calif.: Stanford University Press, 1962).

3. Paul R. Pillar, "Pressuring the Intelligence on Iraq," *Foreign Affairs,* March/April 2006.

4. Final Report of the Iraq Survey Group, July 2005, p. 9.

9. THE CIA IN TRANSITION

1. Christopher Andrew, with Vasili Mitrokhin, *The Sword and the Shield* and *The World Was Going Our Way* (New York: Basic Books, 1999 and 2005, respectively).

10. INTELLIGENCE REFORM

1. The House Committee chaired by Representative Otis Pike (D-N.Y.) attempted to issue its report but the committee failed to vote it out. It later appeared in a leak to the *Village Voice*.

2. After a mix-up surrounding the original covert action in 1981 to support the Nicaraguan Contras, in which it appeared the president did not execute the finding until *after* the covert action had begun, Congress made it clear by statute that the finding had to be in writing and executed *before* the operation began.

3. For example, President Carter chose not to give Congress prior notification of the aborted Desert One operation in 1980 to rescue the American hostages from the U.S. Embassy in Tehran. Congress appeared to accept this decision because of the sensitivity in the timing of the operation.

4. The "gang of eight" was established as a fail/safe device when the executive wanted to severely restrict congressional notification of particularly sensitive covert actions under Hughes-Ryan and succeeding statutes. The eight are the chairman and ranking members of the two intelligence oversight committees, the speaker and minority leader of the House of Representatives, and the majority and minority leaders of the Senate. However, this process was only intended to apply for a short period of time, not for the life of a covert action like the NSA warrantless surveillance.

11. ACTIONABLE INTELLIGENCE AND THE ROLE OF LAW ENFORCEMENT, THE MILITARY, AND TECHNOLOGY

1. It appears that many critical functions at the NCTC are now filled by contractors, either drawn from the retired ranks of the IC or from the private sector. This will do little to build a long-term cadre of counterterrorist specialists.

2. Gary C. Schroen, *First In: An Insider's Account of How the CIA Spearheaded the War on Terror in Afghanistan* (New York: Ballantine Books, 2005); and *Jawbreaker* by Gary Berntsen (New York: Crown Books, 2005).

12. FOREIGN LIAISON SERVICES AND SPYING LAWFULLY

1. See especially Steve Coll, *Ghost Wars* (New York: Penguin Books, 2005).

2. Analysis and Recommendations, Report of the Commission of Inquiry into the Actions of Canadian Officials in Relation to Maher Arar, vol. III (Ottawa, 2006), p. 157.

3. According to the Arar report, ibid., Commissioner O'Connor had invited the United States to give evidence to the commission of inquiry, which it refused to do. In addition, U.S. authorities reviewed the flawed Canadian evidence on Arar with RCMP officials but did not inform them of their intention to remove him to Syria. They simply asked whether the Canadians could hold Arar if he were returned to Canada from New York, and they were told no, the evidence was insufficient. Vol. III, p. 158ff.

4. Ibid., vol. III, p. 159.

5. *One Issue, Two Voices,* no. 6, published by the Canada Institute of the Woodrow Wilson International Center for Scholars, Washington, D.C., January 2007, Statement by Robert Henderson on p. 4.

6. Judicial authorities in Italy and Germany have recently subpoenaed CIA officials to appear in court to answer questions about the

alleged kidnapping of an Egyptian cleric off the streets of Milan and a German citizen in Macedonia.

7. David Luban, "Liberalism, Torture, and the Ticking Bomb," *Virginia Law Review,* vol. 91 (September 2005):1425.

13. UPDATING OPERATIONAL AND ANALYTICAL TRADECRAFT

1. *Washington Post,* April 15, 2007, p. A-9.

14. A SPY FOR THE TWENTY-FIRST CENTURY

1. Tony Judt, *Postwar: A History of Europe Since 1945* (New York: Penguin Press, 2005).

Index